PROCEEDINGS

OF THE

CONVENTION

OF THE

NORTHERN LINES OF RAILWAY,

HELD AT BOSTON,

IN DECEMBER, 1850, AND JANUARY, 1851.

BOSTON:
J. B. YERRINTON & SON, PRINTERS,
NO. 21 CORNHILL.
1851.

PROCEEDINGS

OF THE

CONVENTION

OF THE

NORTHERN LINES OF RAILWAY,

HELD AT BOSTON,

IN DECEMBER, 1850, AND JANUARY, 1851.

BOSTON:
J. B. YERRINTON & SON, PRINTERS,
NO. 21 CORNHILL.
1851.

The undersigned herewith present a Report of the Proceedings of the Railroad Convention, held in this city, in December and January last.

THOMAS THACHER,
WALDO HIGGINSON, } *Committee.*
S. M. FELTON,

PROCEEDINGS.

At an informal meeting of some of the several persons interested in the lines of Railroads leading to Vermont, holden at 11½ Tremont Row, Nov. 13th, 1850, E. Fairbanks, Esq., was appointed Chairman, and S. M. Felton, Esq., Secretary.

It was *Voted*, that a Committee be appointed to call a meeting of the Directors and Superintendents of the Railroads, constituting the several lines of Railway between Boston and Lake Champlain, by way of Concord, N. H., and Fitchburg, Mass., together with the Directors and Superintendents of such connecting lines as it may seem expedient to the Committee to have represented at said meeting, for the purpose of taking means to regulate the competition now existing between portions of said lines, and to consider such other matters as may be brought before them.

It was also *Voted*, to appoint the following a Committee to call said meeting:—

THE PRESIDENT of the Boston & Maine Railroad.
" " Boston & Lowell Railroad.
" " Fitchburg Railroad.
" " Vermont & Mass. Railroad.
" " Sullivan Railroad.

THOMAS THACHER, Esq., of the Cheshire Railroad.

B. T. REED, Esq., of the Ogdensburg Railroad.

NATHAN RICE, Esq., of the Rutland and Burlington Railroad.

Dr. WM. J. WALKER, of the Northern Railroad.

J. P. PUTNAM, Esq., of the Vermont Central Railroad.

JOSIAH STICKNEY, Esq., of the Concord Railroad.

THOMAS S. WILLIAMS, Superintendent of the Boston & Maine Railroad.

WALDO HIGGINSON, Agent of the Boston & Lowell Railroad.

S. M. FELTON, Superintendent of the Fitchburg Railroad.

In accordance with the above vote, invitations were sent by the above Committee to the Presidents, Directors and Superintendents of the following Railroads, requesting them to meet at the Fitchburg station, in

Boston, on Tuesday, December 10th, 1850, at 10 o'clock, A. M.: —

Boston and Lowell,
Nashua and Lowell,
Concord,
New Hampshire Central,
Boston, Concord and Montreal,
Concord and Claremont,
Contoocook Valley,
Northern,
Connecticut and Passumpsic,
Vermont Central,
Vermont and Canada,
Ogdensburg,
Sullivan,
Rutland and Burlington,
Cheshire,
Fitchburg,
Boston and Maine,
Vermont and Massachusetts.

In accordance with this notice, the Convention assembled at the time appointed, in the room of the Directors of the Fitchburg Railroad, in Boston.

The meeting was called to order by JOSEPH TILDEN, Esq., of Boston, who nominated JACOB FORSTER, Esq., of Boston, as President, *pro tem.*

THOMAS S. WILLIAMS, Esq., of the Boston & Maine Railroad, was elected Secretary, *pro tem.*

Messrs. CHARLES THOMPSON, URIAH CROCKER, and THOMAS M. EDWARDS, were appointed, on motion of one of the delegates, by the President *pro tem.*, to retire and nominate a list of officers for the Convention. This

Committee subsequently reported the following list of officers:—

PRESIDENT.

HON. ERASTUS FAIRBANKS, St. Johnsbury, Vt.

VICE PRESIDENTS.

JOHN HOWE, Esq., of Boston.
MR. THOMAS WHITTEMORE, of Cambridge.
DANIEL ABBOTT, Esq., of Nashua, N. H.
JAMES C. DUNN, Esq., of Boston.

SECRETARIES.

S. M. FELTON.
CHARLES F. GOVE.
JOHN R. BREWER.
L. TILTON.

The report was unanimously adopted, and the gentlemen named were requested to act, and took their seats as officers accordingly.

On motion of Mr. FELTON, it was *Voted*, that a Committee be appointed by the President to retire and report what course of proceedings would best promote the objects of the Convention; and that the same Committee remain as a standing Business Committee during the session of the Convention; and that all questions proposed for general discussion be referred to the said Committee, to report upon the expediency of their occupying the time of the Convention.

On this Committee, the President appointed Messrs. J. B. French, Thomas Thacher, S. M. Felton, Waldo Higginson, N. G. Upham, L. Tilton, and John P. Putnam.

The Committee reported as follows:—

REPORT.

That a Committee of Conference be appointed on the part of the roads immediately interested, upon the subject of the competition now existing between White River Junction and Boston via Concord, N. H., and Fitchburg, Mass., and that this Committee consist of a delegate from each of the following Roads, to be appointed by the representatives present from each of these Roads, who shall report the name of said delegate to the President of this Convention as soon as practicable; and the President is requested to announce the Committee to the Convention, when thus completed:—Sullivan, Vermont and Massachusetts, Fitchburg, Cheshire, Rutland, Vermont Central, Connecticut and Passumpsic Rivers, Northern, Concord, Nashua and Lowell, Boston and Lowell, and Boston and Maine. Also, that a Committee be appointed by the President to consider and report the best mode in which the Convention can consider and act upon the subject of the competition now existing between Lake Champlain and Boston, by the way of the Vermont Central and the Rutland and Burlington Railroads.

The Committee farther propose the following:—To consider and act upon the reports of the two Committees already provided for, in the order in which they may be made, and that said reports be always the first in the order of the day until disposed of, unless it be at any time decided otherwise by the Convention; and that the time not occupied by the consideration of these reports, be devoted to the discussion of, and action upon, such other subjects of interest to the Railroads represented as may be deemed expedient; and each subject duly reported for discussion shall be placed upon the order of the day, and considered in turn.

And in order at once to bring the Convention to the consideration of questions of interest and importance, the Committee propose the four following subjects for its attention:—

First. The expediency of increasing the present rates for passengers and freight, and the course of action best calculated to afford a permanent continuance of remunerative rates.

Second. The best mode of increasing efficiency in the transaction of joint business, by improving harmony and union between the several roads concerned in such joint business.

Third. The expediency of the system of excursion trains, at cheap rates.

Fourth. The best method of regulating competition in general, between the several lines of Railroads here represented, both in through and way business.

The Committee farther propose that (in consideration of the importance of having one and the same Secretary throughout all the proceedings of this Convention, and of the other necessary avocations of the gentlemen appointed to act as Secretaries) WILLIAM P. PARROTT, Secretary of the New England Association of Railroad Superintendents, be employed as one of the Secretaries of this Convention; also, that JOSEPH H. BUCKINGHAM be employed as Reporter of the proceedings of this Convention.

This Report was unanimously accepted, and the Convention being fully organized, proceeded to business.

Mr. IRA GOODALL moved the following:—

Resolved, That a Committee be appointed to establish the weights of all such freight as goes by tale or by the ton, and designate which shall go as first and which as second-class.

Under the Rule adopted in the first vote, on motion of Mr. Felton, this Resolution was referred to the Business Committee.

On motion of Mr. Thompson, of the *Sullivan* Road, it was

Voted, That the Committee to be appointed on the subject of the competition now existing between White River Junction and Boston, consist of *two* from each of the Roads mentioned, instead of *one*, as was provided in the Report of the Business Committee.

The President announced the following as the Committee to consider and report on the subject of the competition between the Rutland and Burlington and the Vermont Central Road, being Committee No. 2:

Hon. William Sturgis, of Boston.
Hon. Charles Paine, " Northfield, Vt.
John Howe, Esq. " Boston.
Jacob Forster, Esq. " "
Thomas M. Edwards, Esq., of Keene, N. H.
Dr. William J. Walker, " Boston.
Isaac Spaulding, Esq., of Nashua, N. H.
Hon. Timothy Follett, " Burlington, Vt.
Josiah Stickney, Esq. " Boston.
Josiah B. French, Esq. " Lowell.
Nathan Rice, Esq. " Boston.

Subsequently, Messrs. Edwards and Rice were excused, and Thomas Thacher, Esq., of Boston, and John

A. CONANT, Esq., of Rutland, were substituted in their places on the Committee. At a later period in the forenoon, Mr. CONANT asked and obtained leave to retire from the Committee, in consequence of other engagements; and JOHN P. PUTNAM, Esq., of Boston, was, on motion of Mr. HOWE, appointed to fill the vacancy. The Committee, as finally constituted, consisted of Messrs. STURGIS, PAINE, HOWE, FORSTER, THACHER, WALKER, SPAULDING, FOLLETT, STICKNEY, FRENCH, and PUTNAM.

On motion of Mr. SPAULDING, of the *Concord* Road, it was

Voted, That the members of the above-named Committee be authorized to call, temporarily, on a member of the Board of Directors to which he belongs to supply his place, if he should be necessarily absent; but that he shall himself remain a member of the Committee, and be responsible as such.

On motion of Mr. THOMPSON, of the *Sullivan* Road, it was

Voted, That the same rule be adopted in regard to the members of the Committee to be appointed on the subject of the competition now existing between White River Junction and Boston.

The PRESIDENT then called on the delegates from the different roads interested, to nominate the members of the Committee of Conference upon the subject of the competition now existing between White River Junction and Boston via Concord, N. H., and Fitchburg, Mass.

The following was then reported and announced by the PRESIDENT as the Committee — being Committee No 1:

SULLIVAN — Charles Thompson and David A. Gage.

CHESHIRE — Salma Hale and Lucian Tilton.

VERMONT & MASSACHUSETTS — Thomas Whittemore and D. S. Jones.

FITCHBURG — Jacob Forster and S. M. Felton.

NORTHERN, N. H. — Joseph B. Walker and Onslow Stearns.

CONCORD — Isaac Spaulding and N. G. Upham.

NASHUA & LOWELL — Jesse Bowers and Charles F. Gove.

BOSTON & LOWELL — William Sturgis and Waldo Higginson.

BOSTON & MAINE — Southworth Shaw and Thomas S. Williams.

The President announced that the Business Committee had proposed the following resolution for discussion, and that this was the order of the day for debate:

Resolved, That it is expedient to raise the price for transportation, both of passengers and freight.

Mr. WHITTEMORE, of the *Vermont and Massachusetts Railroad*, said that, so far as concerned the Railroads commencing fifty miles or more from Boston, they *must* either raise their rates on freight and passengers, or do something else to obtain an income, or else they must die. It was well known that the rates on freight throughout the country traversed by Railroads, were very much less now than before they were built; less than the roads could afford to receive, and much less than the freight could afford to pay. Change was not so much needed as to roads terminating in Boston, as in regard to those in the remote country towns; but it was clear to him that, at the present prices, the distant roads must, as a class, be ruined. The result of such a change might be thought uncertain; but without such change, there could be no dividends. He was in hopes that it would be one effect of the present Convention to declare the existing rates on freight to be far too low. Doubtless the newspapers always will advocate low freights and low fares, and these might do well enough for roads near Boston. Some roads could afford a different policy from others. It was well known that fares had been recently raised on the Fitchburg Road, and he had heard little complaint; he thought this a safe precedent. He would vote for a rise, even should odium follow. It was time to inform the public that Railroad business could not be done at the present prices.

Mr. Derby, of the *Fitchburg Railroad*, asked if the last speaker would go above two and a half cents per mile for passengers, that being higher than the general rates on the New York roads?

Mr. Whittemore replied that the rates for both freight and passengers should be raised to a "living" price; high enough to pay honestly, and well. If two and a half cents would not be enough, let it be three cents. He had no special plan to offer, but this was his theory of the case.

Mr. Fairbanks, of the *Connecticut and Passumpsic Rivers Railroad*, supposed the resolution only intended to elicit discussion. The two questions, as to freight and passengers, should be separately considered.

Passengers might so increase in numbers under low freights as to avoid loss. Not so with freights. Some freights would decrease in amount if prices were raised, but most would be but little affected. With certain competing roads — roads competing with water communication — there might be difficulty; freight might be lost by too high a rate. But in local districts, without such competition, where there was a certain amount of products to go to market, and a certain amount of articles to go from the city for consumption, there would be no loss by a rate decidedly higher than the present, provided it were lower than the price paid before Railroads were introduced. But the great object now was equalization — people wish to know that all pay alike.

When stockholders invested money, they expected to have a fair remuneration; they expected, in fact, to have more, in consideration of the risk. A satisfactory result might, he believed, be obtained, but only by ample deliberation. For himself, he had no plan to propose, but thought it more important for the Convention to debate the subject of freight than of passengers.

Mr. Howe, of the *Boston and Maine Railroad*, thought this a matter most pertaining to roads distant from the city, and hoped to hear it debated by those interested in such roads.

Mr. Derby agreed in general with both Messrs. Whittemore and Fairbanks. He thought, with the latter, that the distant country towns would not complain of a moderate increase on present prices. The great inquiry was, What would be a remunerating rate, all things considered? He alluded to the ice business of the Fitchburg road, which was a peculiar business, and could be conducted at a high rate per mile, and not be affected by charges on other kinds of freight, because it was peculiar. He thought that if there was any change, it should be in reference to certain articles of freight and on certain roads. As to flour, however, there were now some millions of barrels in Canada seeking a market; and the question was, Could we take that and bring it to Boston, at an increased rate, in the face of the New York competition? Sixty cents a barrel for flour from Ogdensburg to Boston did not materially vary from the rate charged for coal on the Reading Railroad, and the roads from the North were candidates for this freight, as the Reading Railroad was for the carrying of coal. On that line, this very season, there was a year's dividend made in two months, by the transportation of a single article, at a rate as low as that now charged by our roads for flour. He should be sorry to have any action of this Convention drive away from us this important business. The matter was best left to the different roads; uniformity was impossible; each case must be judged by itself.

As to passengers, he thought it an open question whether two or two and a half cents per mile were most lucrative. He knew one road which had lost money this year by raising the fare. Could as much money be earned at three cents per mile as at present rates? It was a question of returns. At present, our rates are from twenty-five to thirty-three per cent. above those in New York, and would it be well to raise them still more? He suggested that a large Committee should be appointed, to consider and report upon this subject.

Mr. Goodall, of the *White Mountains Railroad*, thought we might establish a certain kind of uniformity in prices, by a classification of roads and fares. The rate on passengers near Boston might be two cents per mile; farther off, two and a half cents; still farther, three cents. A proper Committee could easily arrange this. In case of competing roads, the same result could be produced by taking certain parallel links, and establishing an uniformity for these. Much depended on the state of the country traversed by the road, but he thought it would never be safe to exceed three cents per mile. Again, as to freight, there was always new business arising, the price of which must be determined by experience; and, indeed, there would always be different classes and prices for freight. He approved of the Committee proposed.

Mr. Whittemore agreed that we must not put our prices too high; but something must be done for the suffering roads. He could speak for one road, on which the prices paid for a very large department of business did not give a "living." Roads terminating in Boston, like the Lowell and Fitchburg, could do business on lower terms than interior roads. It was competition which was keeping prices down. The last speaker had alluded to competition in Vermont and New Hampshire; but other roads were suffering in the same way. We, of the Vermont and Massachusetts road, feel the evils of competition at both ends of our small road, for we are in the centre, as it were, of the whole trouble, and have to suffer for the sins of both extremities. It would be a great benefit to have an arrangement made, if it could have some permanency, and be felt as binding on both parties.

There must be some discrimination between interior roads and Boston roads. The Fitchburg and the

Lowell roads might carry passengers for two cents per mile; but the Vermont and Massachusetts Railroad could not live on that. We want to make each road to pursue its business fairly, pay its expenses, and neither fear nor need any dishonest or dishonorable tricks.

Mr. THOMPSON said that on the Sullivan Railroad, they were literally doing business for nothing. He was for changing the rates with reference to freight and not to passengers. Freight rates should be increased, and very considerably. The freight between Boston and White River Junction used to be carried for not less than $20 per ton, and was from four days to a week on the road. Then Railroads were built, and before they were sure of the business, it was well to establish low fares. But now they were sure of it, and there should be a fairer division between the road and the public. The question was whether three-quarters of the advantage in time and cost should go to the public, and the roads, in some cases, lose money? Presidents of roads should see that their stockholders were not robbed for the public convenience. Rates might be raised considerably, and the public still get full half the benefit; and stockholders had a right to demand their share.

Mr. FAIRBANKS called the attention of the Convention to a few facts respecting the great business of the West. Undoubtedly, there was a great amount of produce to come thence, and a corresponding amount of freight to be returned. Undoubtedly, the two great lines from Burlington must come in for a share of that business; but to expect them ever to get all, or, at present, even a very great share, would lead to disappointment. There was an interest on Lake Champlain which must always have its share. Should we reduce the fares even below remunerating rates, the Lake interest would still get its share; and the two lines alluded to could not do all, even were the Lake competition removed. Others must come in for a portion of the Western trade, and reduction of rates would for some time be only injurious. If one line reduced, others must, though a mutual agreement might avoid the difficulty; and there was certainly enough for all to do.

He would allude, with some diffidence, to another matter. The Vermont Central and the Rutland and Burlington roads are yet in their infancy, and have neither sufficient furniture nor moving power to do a great deal more than now; nor are they in sufficient repair to do a great increase of work economically. With the Western Railroad, from Albany to Boston, the case was different. That road could double its freight any day, with small trouble or cost, being largely fitted with engines and cars, and having, moreover, been tested by long use. But it was otherwise with the new roads, and the question was whether, with higher rates, there would not still be a business sufficient, at least, at present, for these roads?

The experience of most Railroad Directors is, that the profits of local business are more sure than of through business, and we must beware lest reducing the latter compel us to reduce the former. The local trade will not bear a reduction beyond a certain point, and no plan is judicious which does not take this fact in view.

Mr. Alvah Crocker, of the *Fitchburg Railroad*, did not intend to occupy much time, but thought the subject of great importance. We have invested in these Railroads millions on millions of dollars, and a great portion of the money is at this moment useless to those who invested it, while the public is a gainer. Towns and neighborhoods have been brought to life, without the stockholders receiving even their legal interest. This needs attention, and the proposed Committee is needed. There were many difficulties, some of which bore, at present, very hard upon the Fitchburg track of the lines to Lake Champlain; but he hoped such a Committee would go thoroughly to work.

Mr. Crocker alluded to the remarks of Messrs. Derby and Whittemore, with each of whom he agreed at some points; but he would assure the latter, especially, that if he raised the price of freight too much on his road, (the Vermont and Massachusetts Railroad,) he would drive all the business away. He must be careful and see lest the increase of only half a dollar a ton should transfer freight from that road to the Connecticut River Road. True, the laborer was worthy of his hire, and some of us certainly had got very little hire for our labor, for a few years back; something was needed to be done, but that carefully. An agreement should be made and adhered to, which should bind other roads than those here present.

There was another thing to be settled by this Convention, viz.: as to the principles which should govern as to territorial or border towns — What are they? — To whom do they belong? He would suggest to the Committee to devise some plan on the subject. For himself, he was in favor of marking out territorial divisions. He hoped that this Convention would do great good;

that its influence would be such as to assist the roads to do an honorable and safe business, and one which would yield something to the stockholders.

Mr. Whittemore said, that if he understood the matter correctly, this resolution was only intended to be suggestive, not decisive. It was a question yet to be decided, whether there was any need of raising prices at all. If not, let us say so, and so much of our business will then be done. *Our* principal competition is from roads not here represented; and they are not here because, although the subject of inviting all the roads was debated in the primary meeting, it was supposed that the first evils to be corrected were those arising from the competition between the rival routes from Lake Champlain to Boston. This Convention was partly an experiment, and might lead, if desired, to a more general Convention.

Mr. Linsley, of the *Rutland and Burlington Railroad*, thought this but an abstract proposition, which this Convention could not settle. As for the freight accumulated at Ogdensburg, we might get that to-day, perhaps, at our own prices; but perhaps to-morrow might tell a different story, from the rise of some new competition.

Mr. Gove moved to lay the Resolution on the table, and this motion was *carried.*

Some conversation arose as to the expediency of an afternoon session, and finally, on motion of Mr. Gove, the Convention adjourned to 3, P. M.

AFTERNOON SESSION.

The Convention was called to order by the President.

Mr. Gove, of the Nashua and Lowell Railroad, regretted that members were not more punctual. He had hoped for a full attendance and a full discussion of the question of the morning. Gentlemen do not seem to realize the importance of the subject. It seemed to him, that the destiny of the Railroad interest depended upon our action at this time. We must resolve to change our course of management, or it will soon be too late. The main object *now* seems to be to show a large amount of *business* done, without regard to the *means* used to get it, or the profits to be derived from it. Means are used to get business from *other roads*, which any one would be ashamed to resort to in the transaction of private business; which shows that the Managers, as well as the Corporations, have but *small* souls, if any. We make solemn bargains with each other to be governed by certain principles and rules, and violate them, the same day, by a secret bargain with an individual, to obtain a small pittance of freight from another road.

The people, seeing this, lose all respect for us, as we seem to have none for ourselves; and they approach us to *dicker* with us, like jockies, without even thinking that we may deem it an insult. In this way, we have already sunk our characters so low, that the term "*Railroad man*" is one of reproach, and at once destroys his influence in legislative halls, and jeopardizes his rights, and the rights of the corporation, even in our courts of justice. No merchant or tradesman could live and deal thus with his neighbors. That great man, "The Public," has thus learned to seize upon us, and to confiscate both us and our roads to his sole use and behoof for ever, as if the stockholders had no rights, and no interests to be protected and looked after. He requires us to make brick even without straw, and if we do not readily submit, he charters another road, that we may fight each other, and thus both become an easy prey to any one who chooses to use us. Our embarrassments are all the effects of our own folly. If we would resolve to do business upon fair and honorable principles, and respect the rights of others, we should be respected, and give little hope of gain by competition. The people are willing to pay a fair and equitable price for doing business well, if we would ask it, like honorable men. Those who make gain by chaffering with us, despise us for it. Mr. Gove referred to several instances of bad faith among Railroad managers, which he characterized as any thing but honorable, and hoped this Convention would do something to put a stop to such proceedings, or the result, in his opinion, would be, to drive every man of honorable feelings out of the business, and leave it to those of a different character; which would be to destroy, not only the interests of stockholders, but the safety and convenience of the public.

A number of members having come in during Mr. Gove's remarks, he called up the Resolution which was laid on the table, and moved its reference to a Committee. The local fare on his road (the Nashua and Lowell) was two and three-quarter cents, which he thought quite as much as it would bear, or more. The through fare was two and a quarter cents. Some thought that this would bear raising, and some otherwise.

It was moved that the Resolution be referred to a Committee of one from each corporation.

Mr. Higginson, of the *Boston and Lowell Railroad*, thought that there would be likely to be a more speedy report, if it were referred to a Committee of three only.

Mr. Thompson expressed great interest in the subject, and hoped it would lead to some action. He had no doubt that if the management of all the roads could be left to the President of the Convention, they would all prove good paying stock; or, if they all belonged to one man, it would be so; the difficulty was in the variety of management, and in the competition. He thought a large Committee could, by a comparison of views, come at the best result.

Mr. Higginson moved to amend by substituting a Committee of three. He thought the discussion in the body of the Convention had elicited a variety of views, on which such a Committee could act understandingly, and that this Committee need not, therefore, be a large one.

Mr. Goodall hoped that one consequence of this Convention would be to diminish the vehemence of competition. He thought, with Mr. Thompson, that were all the roads under one skilful management, they would all pay well. This, of course, was impossible; yet, if any two parallel roads would join and "stock their hands," as was the phrase in staging matters, he believed the stockholders would gain by it. It was astonishing to hear what an amount of business was being offered to us from the great Canada trade. Six hundred thousand barrels of flour, besides other freight, for this year! He did not mean to say that we should not make some exception from other business, in order to get this freight in favor of the Ogdensburg road. All felt an interest in this matter. In 1826, he was present at a meeting for devising measures to facilitate the passage of freight up and down the valley of the Connecticut. Various measures were proposed, but he advised them all to wait for a Railroad. There were then no Railroads in this country, and it was thought a dreamy project. He preferred the larger Committee suggested.

Mr. HIGGINSON then withdrew his amendment. The question being on the motion to refer, as above,

Mr. DERBY advocated it. He stated that there was a commission now sitting in this city of gentlemen from Canada, New Brunswick, Nova Scotia and Washington, on the trade between the British Provinces and the United States. He read a memorandum of statistics respecting the trade, showing its continual increase, and that it is now nearly as large to Europe via the United States, as that by the way of Montreal and Quebec, and bid fair to be soon much larger. He read this to show, not only that the trade was increasing, but that it was possible and important to secure it to Boston. He thought that we could always retain it, even at a higher rate than the New Yorkers, by adopting a liberal policy. Thus far, by our Railroads, we have brought only enough (and sometimes hardly enough) of produce to supply the local trade or consumption. We can sail our ships cheaper than they can be sailed from the South and from New York. All that is needed to increase our navigation is to obtain the quantity of freight. Why should we not carry over our roads the through freight now carried by the slow routes of the canals, and by circuitous navigation?

In his morning's remarks, he had shown that in Pennsylvania, it had been carried as cheap as at our present prices, to an evident profit, giving a year's dividend in two months. The same fact had been demonstrated in regard to the New York Canals. When he referred to the business of the Vermont Central and the Rutland and Burlington roads, he did not speak of the local retail business alone, but of the whole traffic. To name the local business in comparison with the through, would be to compare the trade of a retail apothecary with that of Lawrence & Co. It was out of the large mass of the business that he wished to secure the profits. He wanted the great trade of the West; and he believed that when the spring opened, the roads could promptly make arrangements to do any amount of business which they could obtain.

He remembered the estimates he had aided in making for the business of the Vermont and Massachusetts Railroad, before it was begun, and they would be realized within a twelvemonth. The depressed state of that enterprise could not be ascribed to low charges, for they were higher than on many successful lines. It was owing to other causes, perhaps unavoidable — harsh legislation, change of route, concealed difficulties, extra cost and sacrifices on land and stock. As respects the lines to the North, he believed that during the winter months, say from November to May, the freights would bear a higher rate; but he preferred to leave the whole matter to a judicious Committee.

The motion to refer to a Committee of one from each road was then agreed to.

Mr. Thompson proposed a Nominating Committee. Mr. Forster thought that this very matter was already in the hands of a Committee, which had under consideration the general subject.

The PRESIDENT suggested the reference of the subject to the former Committee; it was only a question of time —whether that Committee could consider it in season.

After some farther conversation, the Committee was appointed and adopted, as follows — being Committee No. 3:—

CHARLES F. GOVE, (CHAIRMAN,) of the Nashua and Lowell Railroad.

N. A. DAVIS, of the Concord and Claremont Railroad.

SAMUEL BACHELDER, of the Boston and Maine Railroad.

JOHN BRADLEY, of the Rutland and Burlington Railroad.

ONSLOW STEARNS, of the Northern (N. H.) Railroad.

GEORGE DENNY, of the Sullivan Railroad.

S. H. PRICE, of the N. H. Central Railroad.

JOHN C. LEE, of the Passumpsic River Railroad.

WALDO HIGGINSON, of the Boston and Lowell Railroad.

SALMA HALE, of the Cheshire Railroad.

J. A. PORTER, of the Contoocook Valley Railroad.

S. M. FELTON, of the Fitchburg Railroad.

N. G. Upham, of the Concord Railroad.

JAMES MOORE, of the Vermont Central Railroad.

THOMAS WHITTEMORE, of the Vermont and Massachusetts Railroad.

IRA GOODALL, of the White Mountains Railroad.

J. N. ELKINS, of the Boston, Concord and Montreal Railroad.

The President then called up the second subject proposed by the Business Committee for discussion, which was — "The best mode of increasing efficiency in the transaction of business, by improving the harmony and union between the several roads concerned."

Mr. Felton, Chairman of the Committee, explained the course which had been heretofore pursued, and said it had led to several controversies between the different roads. He suggested the expediency of having a Central Board appointed, to whom might be left, in future, all such negotiations. He hoped there would be a full expression of opinion.

Mr. Fairbanks, of the *Passumpsic and Connecticut Rivers Railroad*, said that he was at the preliminary meeting which decided on this Convention. Several crude plans were suggested by the gentlemen there met, but it was agreed to leave them all to be acted upon here. Some thought a Central Board might be appointed, on each of the lines connecting Lake Champlain and Boston, consisting of one from each corporation, with certain powers. No doubt, if practicable, it would be better to have each of these lines made into one corporation; but that being impracticable, it was best to come as near that as possible. Others suggested a salaried agent for each line, with power to look into the local interests of each road, the character of its business, its complaints against others, and whatever else might need adjustment; and with authority either to adjust those difficulties, or to refer them to a Central Board. These agents could also confer with each other at the termini of their respective lines, and much difficulty be undoubtedly avoided.

Mr. Higginson said that he had suggested this

proposition to the Business Committee as one of great importance. It was a subject so new, that much depended upon experiment. He had hoped to hear it discussed; but as the afternoon session was not so full as seemed desirable, he would move its reference to a Committee of one from each road, with the President as its Chairman.

This motion was agreed to, and the subject was accordingly referred to the Committee last appointed, with Hon. ERASTUS FAIRBANKS as Chairman.

Mr. FELTON then moved, and it was carried, that the third subject proposed by the Business Committee (that referring to Excursion Trains) should be assigned for discussion at the opening of the next morning's session.

On motion of the same gentleman, the Convention then adjourned until 10, A. M., of the following day.

SECOND DAY.

(WEDNESDAY, DECEMBER 11, 1850.)

The Convention was called to order by the President. The Journal of yesterday was read and approved. The question first in order was the third proposed by the Business Committee, viz.—"The expediency of the system of Excursion Trains, at cheap rates."

Mr. FELTON said that, for the purpose of bringing

up the question in its regular and proper form, he had prepared and would propose the following: —

Resolved, That Excursion Trains are advisable, under proper regulations, as a means of increasing the revenue of the different lines of Railroads here represented; and that these trains also tend to promote good feeling among those who reside on the several lines.

Mr. Felton said that he did not mean to have it understood that he was in favor of Excursion Trains, as they were managed during the last summer. He was not in favor of carrying passengers fifty miles and back for fifty cents. Many things should be considered in fixing a price for these trains, especially the amount of risk incurred. Every body knows, for instance, that if a passenger be hurt on one of these cheap excursions, he will sue the company, and get all he can in the shape of damages; and this risk and imposition should be paid for. Nor did he approve of long excursions, frequently, to distant parts of the country; but he thought such trains might be beneficial to roads in the immediate vicinity of Boston, provided they were not known too long beforehand. He thought that Excursion Trains, now and then, might be expedient, perhaps, to Lake Champlain, for half the usual price; that is, if the fare to the Lake be six dollars, an occasional excursion might be established both ways, at the same price. Many might go on such an excursion in summer who would not otherwise think of it. For instance: at reduced fares, the route, by way of Lake Champlain, to Niagara Falls and Saratoga, (and this route would be the nearest in time,) would attract many pleasure parties. Many people never went to those places because they could not afford the expense; such would be glad of this opportunity. By such arrangements, the travel might be increased to four times its regular amount. There were several such excursions, last summer, over the Fitchburg Railroad, at too low a price—lower than should be ever allowed again. But that these trains produced many advantages, he was certain. He had carefully observed the faces of travellers, and he was satisfied that those trains brought hundreds of people to Boston, during the last summer, who were entire strangers to the city, and who never would have come but for the low fare.

Then as to another point. It might be supposed by some that these Excursion Trains would be availed of by the regular travellers on the road; but his experience led to a different conclusion. On one occasion, a train brought seventeen hundred and carried the same back, and he took the opportunity to examine the books of the company, and found that there were sold on that day about the average number of tickets, at regular prices. He was satisfied that at least fifteen out of seventeen in that train were never in Boston before. Now, let the country people come to Boston once, and they are sure to come again; they imbibe a relish for city life, which they will gratify. People's tastes and amusements change, and these trains are to the country people a novelty; they will give up their old habit of having local pic-nic parties, and will make up parties to Boston instead, if they can do it at a small expense. This benefits both the Railroads and the city.

Mr. Derby agreed with the last speaker, both that

the system had been beneficial, and that the price had been too low. The price should never be less than one cent per mile. The practice was pursued by the Old Colony Railroad Company. They charged one and a half cents per mile for associations, in 1848 and 1849, and he thought they had materially added to the income of that road, without interfering with any regular business. But the practice was of English origin. In England, the roads had found a good effect produced by running Excursion Trains, even on Sunday, for in consequence of these, the beer shops and gin palaces had been almost deserted. He believed that the average English price for Excursion Trains was rather more than a half-penny a mile, though there were different classes in the same trains. The rate for Excursion Trains was, he thought, half the customary rates, in all the cars.

Mr. PAINE, of the *Vermont Central Railroad*, said that he had never yet experienced any of the advantages of Excursion Trains, but that he had experienced their evils fully, having lost much money by them on his road. If Excursion Trains went from Boston to Montreal, people would go in them and not in the regular trains, and we might as well have these trains once a week; we might as well go down to half a cent a mile on all our trains. The excursions benefitted Boston and Montreal, not the Railroads between. They were very well for military companies and parties of pleasure, on short routes, by the single day, but he would go no farther. People often travelled on these trains at a quarter the usual price, on their regular business. For instance: they would buy Excursion tickets, and go to the limit of their journey, and, not intending to return, would sell their tickets, and pocket the price as so much saved. In this way, tickets were often bought at very reduced rates, and all the roads were losers.

Mr. Alvah Crocker expressed himself in favor of Excursion Trains, under certain limitations; the price should never be less than half the usual fare. But do not, he said, let us bring all the country people to Boston for half price. They have some interest in their local stores. Destroy them, and we lose our freights of merchandise, and the public suffer inconvenience also. He had known persons to go from Fitchburg to Boston, last summer, for forty cents! Let this happen often, and it would ruin the Fitchburg storekeepers. Let the privilege be limited to special occasions and objects, and not happen too often. For this end, let the subject be debated fully.

Mr. Denny, of the *Sullivan Railroad*, agreed with the last speaker as to the effect of excursions on the trade of country towns, and knew for a fact that many went in such trains who would otherwise pay full fares.

Mr. Crocker farther remarked, that these trains were injurious to more distant Railroads, since, when such trains were run from Fitchburg to Boston, people from adjoining towns would come by their own conveyance, before the regular trains, to Fitchburg, and take tickets from there, instead of taking the cars at once; and the same remark would apply to the Worcester, Lowell, and other trunk roads.

Mr. Mussey, of the *Passumpsic River Railroad*, thought there were two sides to the question. We are not, in our country, so well provided with means for these trains as in England, where all the roads have double tracks, and other facilities for extras. There, the excursions are always confined to the trip out and back, and are limited as to time, and never go below half the regular fare. To specify a time in advance would ruin the whole plan, as people would wait for the trains, and the regular trains would suffer. There was no harm in special trains, if desired, but they should not be for long distances, nor advertised long beforehand. In England, they sometimes sell tickets for parties to go out and back within a certain time, by which a family may travel; but no special tickets or trains are allowed to interfere with the regular trade; the tickets are not transferable, and when known to have been transferred, are not received.

Mr. Felton thought that Excursion Trains should undoubtedly be so arranged that the public should not be able to calculate on them beforehand. Nor should they be frequently allowed on the Vermont Central or the Rutland and Burlington roads. Running such trains out of Boston one hundred or one hundred and fifty miles, once or twice a year, he thought might prove beneficial; people who had five dollars to spare might spend it in this way in preference to some other. There should be a limitation, both as to the number of trains and the price; they should not be, as they had been, as often as once a week; one or two a year would be quite enough on the lines with which the Fitchburg road connected. On that road, however, it had always been customary to take military and engine companies, and other special parties, at reduced rates, when there was guarantied a car full—say sixty persons. This had been beneficial both to the Railroad and the public; it had discouraged the spending of money at country taverns in dissipation, and had added to the income of the Railroad. He thought, however, that the Railroads gained more profit by Excursion Trains *from* Boston than *to* Boston; and he still held, in spite of the objections he had heard urged against them, to the desirableness of occasional special trains to convey parties to Montreal, Saratoga, &c., at reduced prices.

As to the remarks of Mr. Mussey, he did not think that single Excursion tickets, or family Excursion tickets, would be of any benefit, unless on such a road as the New York and Erie Railroad, where they might induce travellers to return the same way instead of a different one. All Excursion tickets should be confined to particular trains. One reason why no harm was done to the regular travel on the Fitchburg road, last summer, was that these Excursion Trains could not be depended on to make to time, by business men. There should be the same system adopted, however, on all the roads, and fares should never be reduced beyond one-half.

Mr. Higginson, of the *Lowell Railroad*, felt pleased with the conservative views expressed by gentlemen on this subject, and particularly with those of Mr. Felton. Last summer, Excursion Trains were almost a mania, but experience had checked the excess of the enthusiasm. The terms of the present Resolution were rather vague. "Excursion Trains" was an indefinite term. There had always been a system of Excursion tickets, in one sense, for schools, military companies, &c.; these were proper on all roads. But the whole theory of the Excursions now under consideration was different, and involved great interference with the regular business. So great had this been found, that some roads, as the Worcester, have discontinued the practice.

He thought much more favorably of excursions from Boston than into Boston. But several strong objections had not yet been stated. You must have some system as to these trains, as is admitted; and any system must become known, and passengers designing to go, at any rate, will arrange accordingly, and avail themselves of it.

A yet greater objection is in the effect produced on the public mind as to the proper standard of Railroad fares. It was the opinion of a late Bostonian, distinguished for his wealth and sagacity, that no investment was safe, the income of which depended on a "toll" paid by the public; that, sooner or later, the public would take this subject of tolls into their own hands, and reduce them, directly or indirectly, below remunerative rates. It is from some such general idea as this, doubtless, that Railroads have ceased to be a favorite investment of capitalists. This is not a false fear; and if Excursion Trains are run very often, the opinion will gain ground that half price is enough ordinarily, and that rates should be lowered accordingly. It is for the interest of the public to reduce rates, and this system goes to justify the propriety of its being done. Public opinion has settled that from two to three cents a mile is enough on any road; and let it settle that half that amount is enough, as many legislators in New Hampshire, New York and Massachusetts believe to-day, and, by direct legislation, or, more probably, indirectly, through increased competition, roads will suffer.

Individual instances may occur where a profit of

several hundred dollars may be made on one excursion trip; in certain places and directions, and under certain circumstances, they may be expedient; but, looking forward to the result of a regular system of excursions, we see its dangers.

Gov. Paine, of the *Vermont Central Railroad*, said that the Resolution was far too vague. He had nothing to say as to excursions on the Boston roads, but he must oppose any extension to the country roads. Such a system would at once open the door for a system of half price for every fare. He could not approve the proposed trains from Boston to Montreal.

Mr. Goodall, of the *White Mountains Railroad*, thought the Resolution might be amended and made more acceptable. Many people came into the country, last year, to do business, by these Excursion Trains, who would otherwise have travelled at full fares. The excursions should be limited to one or two a year, and the tickets only be received in those particular trains.

Mr. Felton here offered an amendment, making his Resolution read as follows:—

Resolved, That occasional Excursion Trains, adapted to the circumstances of each case and each road, under proper regulations, are desirable, as a means of increasing the revenue of each road; and that they also tend to promote a good feeling among those residing on the different lines; and that these Excursions should be confined to special trains, and the rates of fare in no case be less than one-half the regular rates.

Mr. Higginson asked Mr. Felton how he proposed to confine Excursion tickets to special trains, when the parties purchasing were allowed to go from Boston to Niagara and back, and be absent for a week?

Mr. Felton replied that he would specify certain days on which the tickets should be good, and make a precise statement on the tickets, and limit them to those days. Nor did he see the force of Mr. Higginson's objection. Business men and business women were obliged to come to Boston once a year, or oftener, to replenish their stock of goods; and it was more important to them to have the goods at the right time, than to make a small saving in fares. The Excursion Trains undoubtedly took some passengers from the regular ones, but they brought a great many who would otherwise have staid at home. He did not fear their prejudicing public opinion against Railroads. Indeed, public opinion had certainly settled in favor of the plan of occasional Excursion Trains. Public opinion is, in the long run, reasonable; people can see the cause for the difference between the charge for carrying a regular train of one hundred and a special train of four hundred passengers. He thought, in fact, that the public would appreciate the spirit of accommodation which led to these Excursion Trains, and for that reason, be more favorably inclined towards Railroads. But the system had been carried too far last summer, and hence been injurious, from its abuses.

Mr. Low, of the *Passumpsic River Railroad*, thought the matter not very hard to settle. The whole profit of Excursions arose from there being *no* fixed system. Each road should arrange them at its own discretion, though never below a certain minimum. He agreed with the views of Gov. Paine.

Mr. J. A. Conant, of the *Rutland and Burlington Railroad*, said that last year we carried passengers as we did cattle, at ruinous rates. He would suggest that Excursion Trains should not have previous notice, especially on one or two parallel roads. But a car full from Brandon or Rutland, to Boston, going and returning on particular days, in special trains, might be advantageous, once in a great while. But he did not approve of extending such trains to Montreal, nor would he ever take less than fifty, or at less than half price.

Gov. PAINE thought the Resolution objectionable, even as modified, though he was not opposed, under all circumstances, to Excursion Trains. He agreed with Mr. Conant's views.

Mr. WHITTEMORE disapproved of the whole system of Excursion Trains. The arguments in their favor were like those for intoxicating drinks—they gave an occasional stimulus, but diminished the vital strength in the end. As he had said before, we had ourselves to blame if our Railroads were not prosperous. People were willing to pay remunerating prices, if demanded; but we had lowered and lowered our rates, till they yielded no profit. He recollected one Excursion Train over the Vermont and Massachusetts Railroad, and back, which carried seventeen hundred persons, and on asking the Superintendent what share the road got, he was told that it averaged *one-quarter of a cent per mile.* [The figures having been calculated by Mr. THACHER, of the *Cheshire Railroad*, he interrupted the speaker to say that the price was *half a cent per mile.*] Even that (proceeded Mr. W.) is ruinous to any road, for any number of passengers; no road could afford even twice that. The Railroads did not begin this practice. It was a speculation of picture dealers and exhibitors of miles of Mirrors; and in the end, *they* got the gold and *we* the copper. The whole system was injurious; and while we complained that prices were too low, we ought not, by this system, to bring them down lower.

Gov. A. Colby, of the *Concord and Claremont Railroad*, said that ten years' experience in staging had shown him where we were getting to stand as to Railroads. He was opposed to the Resolution, and to Excursion Trains. If the sole object was popularity, why not run them once a week for nothing? He once was concerned in running opposition stages on a certain route, and they were run for seven months at a loss of about thirty dollars a day, and the competitors had at last to pocket the loss and join stocks. In Railroads, there should be one fixed price. The stock of our roads was owned chiefly in Boston, and if Boston people wished to use them, let them pay for it. If the system were profitable, why not ask hotel keepers and others to apply it? their experiments would be instructive. There never yet was a stage passenger grateful for getting his fare for nothing, and it would be the same with Railroads. The reason why Railroads were unpopular was because stockholders had been encouraged to expect ten per cent. for their money; and they would not regard Excursion Trains or low fares as any substitute for dividends.

Mr. Joseph Low, of the *Concord and Claremont Railroad*, thought there should be no general system, but each road should make its own arrangement.

Mr. William Sturgis, of the *Boston and Lowell Railroad*, supposed the object of this Resolution was not decision, but discussion. In his experience, the public were never grateful for any improper indulgence; nor was there ever a reduction which did not lead to another. One speaker had suggested that if a system were established, it would be violated in a week. Perhaps that was incorrect; but he was sure that a week would not pass before some road would complain that some other road had violated it. He was opposed to the Resolution, even in its amended form.

Gov. Colby moved an amendment, which, however, he withdrew in favor of one offered by Mr. Howe, as follows:—

Resolved, That the following general regulations be adopted in regard to Excursion Trains:

First. That they be confined exclusively to associations, either organized or voluntary, and that the different roads on the line be consulted.

Second. That the price shall never be less than half the regular fares, and that Excursion tickets ought to be confined to Excursion Trains.

Third. That Excursion Trains shall never be advertised by Railroad companies.

This amendment was adopted, without a count. The question then was on the adoption of the Resolution, as amended.

Mr. Higginson remarked on the important concession made by all the speakers, even by the mover of the original Resolution, as to the necessity of some limitation on the practice of Excursion Trains. He feared, however, for the effect of these trains during the next summer, if carried out as proposed. They would interfere with regular business, and bring blame as well as embarrassment to the executive of the roads.

The dangers ascribed to them had been admitted, to some extent, to-day. Gentlemen had admitted that Railroad fares depended somewhat on public opinion. He thought that if any system of this kind were adopted, it could not afterwards be discontinued, because the public, the great contracting party, was sufficiently powerful to prevent it, and would hold the Railroads, which were the weaker party, to what they had themselves set the example of granting.

Mr. WHITTEMORE, of the *Vermont and Massachusetts Railroad*, called for a division of the question, which made the question before the Convention to be on adopting the first proposition, viz.:—

"That they [Excursion Trains] be confined exclusively to associations, either organized or voluntary, and that the different roads on the line be consulted."

Messrs. WHITTEMORE and HOWE had some conversation as to the meaning of the word "associations," in the Resolution, which was finally explained to include all companies of persons who had a plan matured for an excursion before making application to the Railroad.

Mr. SAWYER, of the *Passumpsic River Railroad*, thought that Excursion Trains might be advantageously run to and from agricultural conventions, cattle fairs, &c., in the country towns.

Mr. DENNY, of the *Sullivan Railroad*, thought this class might be indefinitely enlarged, and that the rule should be so amended as to be limited to organized societies. He was not in favor of conveying the public at lower rates to any and every public gathering.

GOV. COLBY agreed with this.

Mr. DENNY then moved a farther amendment:—

"That Excursions should be confined to each individual Railroad corporation."

His object was to avoid one difficulty, and provide that no road should bind any other road.

Mr. STURGIS thought that there was no danger of this, since no one road could possibly bind another. If an Excursion covers several roads, they must all be consulted.

After some farther conversation on this point, of rather a desultory character, in which Messrs. DENNY, STURGIS, COLBY, W. F. WELD, NATHAN RICE, LOW and CONANT took part, and in which slight amendments were offered and withdrawn,

Mr. HIGGINSON moved to lay the first proposition on the table. The second would establish a principle, which was a good deal for one day.

This motion was agreed to, without a count.

The next question was on adopting the second proposition:—

"Second. That the price shall never be less than half the regular fares, and that Excursion tickets should be confined to Excursion Trains."

Mr. THACHER moved to lay this upon the table, which motion was opposed by Messrs. HIGGINSON and LOW, and rejected.

Mr. STURGIS moved, and it was voted, to insert the words "rates of" before "fares." The second proposition, thus amended, was adopted.

The question was then on adopting the third proposition:—

"Third. That Excursion Trains shall never be advertised by Railroad companies."

And this was agreed to, without debate, unanimously.

The PRESIDENT announced that the first subject in order for discussion was now that of the Rates of Fare for Cattle Trains.

On motion of Mr. THOMPSON, the Convention adjourned to 3, P. M.

SECOND DAY—AFTERNOON SESSION.

The PRESIDENT having called to order, Mr. FELTON, from the Business Committee, reported the following subject for discussion: —

"The expediency of increasing the Rates of Tariff on Cattle Trains."

Mr. STEARNS, of the *Northern Railroad*, said that this business was at present very unprofitable, and that the rates should be raised. This kind of freight was peculiar, as requiring the use of cars which could be employed only in one direction, (towards Boston,) and must go back empty, being dirty and unfit for use.

Mr. ALVAH CROCKER thought the great difficulty lay in the competition on the Northern Railroads, and in the consequent cheapness. Besides the evils suggested by Mr. Stearns, there were others as great; these trains must almost always run out of time, in the night, &c. There was no branch of business benefitted more by Railroads than this, and the difference in the value of the property after transportation would always more than pay the cost of transporting. Again, there was an extra risk on such freight; on almost every such train there was some accident to some animal, and drovers were not usually slow to claim damages.

Mr. STEARNS feared one fact would operate against raising these rates. Drovers know they can obtain higher prices for cattle brought by Railroad, and they will be likely to drive them nearly to their destination, and then take the cars.

Mr. FELTON thought it absolutely necessary for this tariff to be increased. The drovers could afford to pay better; the cattle brought higher prices when transported in the cars, and there was no loss from shrinkage. This was the most costly of all freight to Railroads; the cars were always left unfit for any other use, and many such cars must be kept on hand, which must always go back empty. He did not see why the drovers could not pay as much to bring their cattle from Burlington to Boston as from Albany to Boston, but it was quite otherwise. He had the curiosity, a few days ago, to look particularly into this matter. He had sent up two engines to Fitchburg, which brought back a train of cattle; this made a travel equal to two hundred miles. Then the cars were carried back empty, making another hundred miles—in the whole, three hundred; and for all that, the road got but $200. We have to send up engines once a week to Fitchburg, and keep them there, under steam, for several hours, in order to accommodate this particular business. He doubted whether it would not be better to give up the business, than to do it at the present rates. On one occasion, a lot of pigs were brought over this road, and, as he was short of cars for some return freight, he had the cars swept and thoroughly cleansed, and then loaded them with salt. But when the salt arrived, the consignees refused to receive it, on account of its condition;—the pigs, instead of being pickled by the salt, had taken their turn, and put the salt into a pickle. On the Fitchburg road, no cars were furnished for this business; the upper roads provided them.

Mr. BRADLEY, of the *Rutland and Burlington Railroad*, read the following:—

Resolved, That forty dollars be charged for an eight-wheel cattle car from Burlington to Boston, and in the same proportion for intermediate places. Also, that Plaster be taken from Boston to Burlington at three dollars and a half per ton, and in that proportion.

He thought that the more we did of the business, the worse, at present prices.

Mr. GOODALL, of the *White Mountains Railroad*, feared, with Mr. Stearns, that a rise in price would drive away these freights; but agreed, with Mr. Felton, that this would be better than present prices. In some places, the drovers already used the Railroad but part of the way.

Mr. CROCKER suggested an amendment to Mr. Bradley's Resolution. At some seasons, it was not worth so much to the drovers to bring their cattle to market, and then they could drive them without loss. This would apply to two months in a year, and he proposed to Mr. Bradley to except September and October, and raise the price for the other months to forty-five dollars.

Mr. BRADLEY accordingly amended his motion so as to read—"Except for cattle during the months of September and October, when the present rates shall be continued."

He wished to have the rate of freight on Plaster fixed low, as that was an article much used in the country, and about the only one which could be carried, in any quantity, in cattle cars.

Mr. THOMPSON, of the *Sullivan Railroad*, said that the two months excepted were those in which three-fifths of the cattle went over the roads.

Mr. CONANT, of the *Rutland and Burlington Railroad*, thought present prices far too low; but it would never do to have two prices for different seasons.

Mr. THOMPSON moved to strike out the exception.

Mr. GOODALL thought we should not go as high as forty dollars quite yet. He proposed thirty-six dollars for a certain time, as till Nov. 1, and then forty, and moved to amend accordingly.

Mr. CROCKER disagreed, and thought even forty dollars poor pay.

Mr. BRADLEY also opposed the amendment, and it was ultimately withdrawn.

Mr. THOMPSON'S motion to strike out the exception was then passed, unanimously. The question then recurring on the original Resolution,

Mr. CONANT suggested an amendment (accepted by the mover) to include Coal with Plaster in the second clause, as that was also an article now much used, and capable of being carried in cattle cars, and should go cheap.

Mr. HIGGINSON thought it not desirable to settle the matter too decisively until a fuller meeting. He thought the subjects of Plaster and Coal should be kept separate.

Mr. FAIRBANKS, the President, (Mr. HOWE in the

chair,) thought the subjects were properly connected, since it was an object to the roads to avoid sending the cars back empty.

Mr. BRADLEY said that Coal was now brought from New York to the line of the Rutland Railroad, or within its reach, for $2.50 per ton, or even less. He thought that $3.50 was the highest rate which Plaster would bear.

Mr. GOODALL called for a division of the question.

Whereupon the first part, "That forty dollars be charged for an eight-wheel cattle car from Burlington to Boston, and in that proportion for intermediate places," was accepted, without a count.

Mr. HIGGINSON then moved that the second part— that respecting Plaster and Coal—be referred to the Committee on raising fares; which was agreed to, without a count.

The Convention then adjourned to 10, A. M., of the following day.

THIRD DAY.

(THURSDAY, DECEMBER 12, 1850.)

The Journal of yesterday having been read and approved,

Mr. BIGELOW, of the *Rutland and Burlington Railroad*, offered the following:—

Resolved, That the same fare ($40 per car) be charged on cattle, as far as Vergennes, on the Rutland

Railroad, and as far east as Waterbury, on the Central Railroad.

On motion of Mr. GOODALL, this was referred to the Business Committee.

On motion of Mr. GAGE, of the *Sullivan Railroad*, the Convention took a recess until twelve o'clock.

At 12, M., the Convention was called to order by the President.

Mr. STURGIS, from the Committee on the competition between the Rutland and Burlington and the Vermont Central Railroads, reported verbally that the suggestion for an arrangement had been met in the most cordial manner, and that there was a reasonable prospect that an arrangement would be made. The Committee were proceeding in the matter, and would report in due time.

Mr. HIGGINSON, from the Committee on the best mode of increasing the efficiency in the transaction of joint business, by promoting harmony and union between the several roads concerned, reported as follows: —

REPORT.

That a Central Board be established upon each of the great lines between Boston and Lake Champlain, including the connecting roads of each line.

That said Central Boards shall be composed of one delegate from each road on said lines, and be fully authorised to represent the same.

The object and duties of said Boards shall be to consider and consult upon all matters relating to the joint business of the associated roads, and to adopt such regulations and decisions as may be expedient for the general interests of said roads.

It being understood, that the action of said Boards shall in no case bind the Directors of any road, without the consent of the delegate from that road.*

Said Boards shall hold their first meeting at a place to be designated by this Convention, and shall be duly organized. Their subsequent meetings shall be on call.

On motion of Gov. Paine, this Report was laid on the table. Judge Gove, for the Committee to whom was referred the subject of raising the prices for transportation, offered the following Report (in part):—

REPORT.

That, in the opinion of the Committee, the present rates on many articles between Boston and Lake Champlain are not remunerative, and that, in adjusting a tariff between these points, reference should be had to the water communication between Burlington and Albany, and the Railroad communication between Albany and Boston; † but not to the cost of transportation between Burlington and New York. Thus, if the freight from Burlington to Boston, via Western Railroad, is $6.00 per ton, a little more than that may be charged by Railroad directly to Boston. But if the rate from Burlington to New York is but $3.00 per ton, it is the opinion of your Committee, that this affords no reason why the rates by Railroad to Boston should be diminished below a remunerating price.

The Railroads have an advantage over water communication, both in time and certainty, of which they

* See page 62 for an amendment subsequently passed.

† See amendment subsequently passed.

should avail themselves by charging an enhanced price. Your Committee would therefore recommend, that on all freight centering at Burlington, regard be had only to such competition via Western Railroad, except in case of the freight that comes over the Ogdensburg Railroad, (either by the Vermont and Canada or other Railroads, or by water communication.) On this freight to and from the great West, it may be advisable to adopt a somewhat lower tariff in regard to some articles, because it is supposed that the quantity will be very great both ways, and thus, although the *per centage* of profit may be small, the aggregate will be large. In their opinion, however, it will not be advisable, even here, to adopt so low a scale as by water communication, nor a scale so low as to leave a doubt as to the existence of some actual profit.

Mr. Goodall moved the acceptance of this Report.

Mr. Upham, of the *Concord Railroad*, was glad to hear from Mr. Sturgis his verbal report, that some arrangement was likely to be made on the subject referred to. He was also glad to hear the last Report, but suggested the inquiry, whether action upon it might not be premature, as obstructing the proceedings of the other Committee.

Mr. Sturgis replied, that the plan proposed between the Vermont Central and the Rutland Railroads would not require any tariff of prices to be made by this Convention, as the two roads would make such arrangements as were mutually advantageous. He hoped they would adopt the general principle of not taking any freight below remunerating prices. But in Committee, the matter of prices had not yet come up, because, if there were an agreement, there would be no more competition.

He approved the general views of this Report.

How far the question of water communication should be taken into account, he did not know. He had heard some gentlemen express the opinion that it might be expedient to do business at present without any actual profit, in order to increase the quantity and gain the trade; but on this subject, he was not decided in his own mind.

Judge FOLLETT, of the *Rutland and Burlington Railroad*, presented a copy of the tariff of prices adopted by his road, and said it was prepared after due consideration, and with a fair understanding that both the roads from Lake Champlain to Boston should be bound by it. This printed tariff was not the first effort; he believed it was the result of the third attempt at a proper standard. The roads were yet in their infancy, and could not yet judge as to the permanent rates; but he thought this sufficiently correct for the present.

He explained some of the items of the tariff, and spoke of the *second-class* freight especially, on which there was a clause allowing, under some circumstances, a discount of twenty per cent. The articles of this class were numerous, and the amount large, and experience alone could prove whether a proper discrimination had always been made.

But he wished to speak more especially to another point. The Rutland Railroad had its terminus on Lake Champlain, where it could connect with the business of the North and South. In establishing these rates of freight, it was necessary to consider all the circumstances of that business. The first tariff they had adopted, and the second also, had successively proved too high; with the present one, they got all they could do, and he believed it was the same with the Vermont Central Railroad. The prices by the way of Albany to Boston were decidedly lower than by these two direct lines. Now, this Report, as he understood, said that the rates via Albany should not be regarded. Gov. Paine had stated that he had had Railroad iron carried for $3.25 per ton, by water communication, from Boston. There was much freight carried to Lake Champlain or to Montreal, the owners of which were in no hurry. A trader could carry home a single hogshead of molasses, or a small quantity of any such article, for immediate necessities, and could easily wait to have the rest come slowly by water, to save something in freight.

It was a difficult thing to arrange a tariff, and they had been obliged to consult Mr. Felton and others. The Rutland Railroad ran for sixty miles near the Lake, and when produce came to Burlington, it was doubtful whether it would go on to Whitehall or by the Railroad to Rutland. Middlebury (thirty miles from Burlington) had always employed water communication; Brandon (fifty miles distant) had always had a direct connection with the Lake; and it was important to obtain the trade of those towns. He was opposed to any increase in rates of freight.

Mr. Felton agreed, to some extent, with the last speaker. No doubt the rates via Albany were less on some articles, but on others they were higher than on the Vermont Central and Rutland Roads. He supposed that this Report did not contemplate a reference to the water communication all the way from Lake Champlain to Boston, for there were not many articles calculated to go by such a route. As for the lot of iron alluded to as having been transported so cheap, the company for which it was carried happened to be able to wait two or three months without difficulty. But the business of traders was changing rapidly. Merchants bought smaller stocks and replenished them oftener, and could afford to pay higher freight, to avoid delay.

He supposed the object of the Convention to be to induce these companies to revise their rates of freight. He spoke of the article of Oats, as one embraced in an uncertain business, a few days often making a difference of several cents in a bushel in the market price, which would justify a higher rate of freight; and so with Butter and Cheese, the market price of which is constantly changing. If a merchant went to Canada for produce or with goods, he would not run the risk of water communication all the way; because the difference in time is worth more than the saving on the freight. So also with Flour, on which insurance was quite an item of expense, which merchants would pay something to reduce; to say nothing of the advantage in speed, &c. He thought there had been too much anxiety on the part of these roads to obtain business, without waiting till the public called for lower prices.

Judge Follett said that, if left to themselves, Oats would never get to Boston at all; and so with Butter, Cheese, &c. When the owners come down the Lake to Burlington, if they find the freight by water cheap, they push on to New York; and if the articles stay there, the roads have lost the freight. New York is a formidable competitor; and a great deal of produce starts without any designated market, and the owners go where they can sell to the best advantage. We must make it their interest to stop at our terminus.

He doubted whether the roads had been too anxious

to obtain business. They cannot lie idle. They have several objects, one of which is to develop business. He spoke of Marble as a great staple on the Rutland Railroad, and one which would not come to Boston except at a low freight, since New York was a great market for it, and speed was no object.

Mr. FELTON thought Railroads in general were too anxious for business. But the course of trade had changed. Formerly, there were great quantities of freight sent down to the great store-houses, to be pushed forward to a market as soon as possible, before the navigation closed. This was not now the case. People used to be obliged to carry freight to market, and there store, to wait for a rise in price, since, if the owners kept their produce at home until the spring, they feared a glut in the market, and a consequent loss. As to the Boston market, he had been told that Flour was generally from ten to twenty-five cents a barrel higher there than in New York. So it was with Cheese, Butter and Oats. Boston was also represented as a safer market than New York; a fact which we should take advantage of, and charge higher freight. No doubt many articles would not bear higher rates than those now charged, but he thought that many others would.

He referred again, in conclusion, to the Cattle business, and said that since the remarks made yesterday, he had some doubts whether it was an object to do it at the rates now agreed upon.

Mr. FAIRBANKS, the President, (Judge FOLLETT in the chair,) thought the local business was the life of all roads, and the through business should never be allowed to interfere with it. He thought the two roads in question had sought such a tariff as would secure the business and not destroy themselves. He remembered the former trade with Montpelier; it was all done by eight-horse teams, and but few articles were sent by way of the Lake. So it was with many other towns, on both routes, which had greatly increased their trade.

He referred to different articles mentioned in the tariff, and objected to the twenty per cent. discount, giving illustrations of its tendency, by comparing and calculating figures;—that on second-class freights, entitled to twenty per cent. discount, the rate per ton between Waterbury and Boston—two hundred and fifteen miles—was $4.80;—that the rate between Ludlow (on the Rutland Road) and Boston—one hundred and forty-four miles—was (he thought) $3.92; while the minimum rate between White River Junction and Boston—one hundred and forty-two miles—was $5.40. He farther stated, that there existed an agreement between the Passumpsic and lower roads for a division of proceeds of freight, to which agreement he had supposed the Central was a party;—that this agreement was specific, each of the roads below White River Junction being entitled to a specific sum per ton; and that, if the Vermont Central settled with the lower roads on the same terms as the Passumpsic, then all which would remain to the Central Road on this class of freights between Waterbury and Boston, would be 80½ cents per ton;—that he had no means of knowing what proportion the Rutland road received in their division of joint freights. He did not see how a change in prices, and more discrimination, could affect the local business, and thought there was room for some improvement. He did not see how the freight on

Marble, which was purely a local trade, should affect or be affected by any other. All these particular points should be considered in arranging a tariff, taking care, above all things, not to injure the local trade.

Moreover, there had not yet been time to develop all the resources of the country on the lines of different roads, and we must wait to see the effects of the new avenues. He spoke of the article of Copperas, which was carried over his road, and the transportation of which could not affect any other article. So with Marble, on the Rutland Railroad. Lumber, from his neighborhood, used to go down the Connecticut; but he and others thought it could command higher prices on their Railroad, so they put the price higher. There was great complaint among the lumber men, and they declared they would never send by that mode; but now they send by the Railroad altogether.

Judge Follett thought the tariff might be revised in regard to many towns on the road. In establishing the rates for through freight, it was understood that towns on the road should have their freight carried at proportionate rates, and he instanced Ludlow as a point where there might be a revision in prices; and many other towns might pay more. Local freight paid about five cents a mile, generally. As to Lumber, he thought the road spoken of might have the advantage of time saved, and protection and safety, over the river routes, and could naturally get higher rates in view of these things.

The debate here ceased, for the present, without any question being taken.

Mr. HIGGINSON moved, and it was

Voted, That the Business Committee be authorised to invite the Presidents, Directors and Superintendents of other roads, not represented in the Convention, to be present this afternoon and to-morrow, and take part in the debate on raising present rates of fare.

The Convention then adjourned to $3\frac{1}{2}$, P. M.

THIRD DAY—AFTERNOON SESSION.

The Convention was called to order by the President, but owing to the small number of delegates present, the debate on the morning's subject was not resumed.

Judge GOVE, from the Committee on raising the prices of transportation, reported verbally that the Committee were preparing their Report, but were not yet ready to offer it.

The Convention then adjourned, to meet on Friday, at 10, A. M.

FOURTH DAY.

(FRIDAY; DECEMBER 13, 1850.)

The Convention was called to order by the PRESIDENT. The Journal of yesterday was read and approved.

The unfinished business of yesterday, being the discussion of the Report on raising fares, was, on motion of Mr. Higginson, laid on the table.

On motion of the same gentleman, the Report of the Committee recommending a Central Board was taken from the table for discussion.

Judge Gove, of the *Nashua and Lowell Railroad*, was surprised at the tenor of the Report in speaking of *Boards;* he thought that it would recommend only the establishment of *one* Board. He did not understand that we had met here to adjust the differences between the members of one line, but between two rival lines. He thought that there had been a perpetual scramble between the different roads in the country, in order to get business, which had been more like horse-jockeying than the conduct of men of business and of honor. Hence the odium of which he had before complained as attaching to "Railroad men." Hence constant quarrels and complaints, and "Investigating Committees," where there was nothing wrong to investigate. Men would tamper with Railroad agents as they would not with any other men, and try every method to coax prices down below a fair rate. He knew a case where a man living within ten miles of the Passumpsic River Railroad, and not nearer than forty miles to any other road, had his goods teamed and carried to the Railroad for nothing. The owner, perhaps, did not know, and certainly did not care, how his goods got there, only that they did get there, with some profit to him. He thought it quite time to stop this business. He, for one, could see the "handwriting on the wall." If such management was not to be prevented, he advised every body of honorable character to get out of Railroads as soon as possible.

He referred to the Report which was discussed yesterday. Why had the Committee suggested any competition with the Western Railroad? What had that to do with Railroads from Lake Champlain? He did not wish it to go to the public that we thought it necessary to suggest a fare to meet the rates of fare on that road. Every road must have its own rate of fare and adhere to it, and roads injudiciously placed must suffer for it. He often saw in the newspapers accounts of the gross amount of tonnage on different roads. These might be correct, but the account of profit and loss was not stated;—no account of the sum paid for teaming, for instance. In the case he had before alluded to, the freight did not net his road one mill; and he doubted if the other roads on the line fared any better. He moved a recommitment of the Report, to amend it by substituting one Board for two.

Mr. Higginson said it was the plan of the Committee that two Boards should be formed, as a preliminary step. Whether or not these should act together, and, under our sanction, make one great Central Board, with legislative powers to settle all differences and determine on prices, was another matter, which they had not ventured to decide.

As to the object of the proposed organization, it was not, as he understood, merely to adjust competition, but to obtain a general harmony, likewise. For instance: the road which he represented was connected with some half dozen between Burlington and Boston, and questions of right and expediency (some very important) were constantly coming up. It would be very desirable to settle them harmoniously, by a Central Board. He preferred the Report as it was. If it was desired to have one general Board, by and by, well and good; but the two Boards must be the first step.

Mr. Denny, of the *Sullivan Railroad*, thought there was some misunderstanding on this point, and read from minutes of the Committee meetings to show that only *one* Board had been there contemplated.

Mr. Higginson thought the affair might be easily settled by moving an amendment.

Mr. Edwards, of the *Cheshire Railroad*, preferred a recommitment, as there was evidently a misunderstanding among the Committee.

Mr. Fairbanks, the President, (Mr. Howe in the Chair,) made some explanations as to the views of the Committee. He thought the Report covered all the ground necessary. Whatever might be the result of a larger organization, it was important to have a smaller one come into it. The two Boards could easily delegate a smaller number to act in their joint business.

Judge Gove did not object to such organization, but thought there ought not to be a separate Board for each line.

Mr. Higginson said that this was the first step to accomplish what Judge Gove desired. We want some body, or Board, to hear complaints and various statements, and this Board might easily delegate power to some smaller body. He thought that any amendment might be made as well here as any where.

Mr. Whittemore thought there was much force in the last remark. He would vote for an amendment, but not for a recommitment.

Judge Gove withdrew his motion to recommit.

Mr. Whittemore (the question now being on accepting the Report) said he liked especially the last clause in the Report, providing that no decision of the Central Board should bind any road without the consent of its delegate.

Judge Gove moved to amend by inserting the following before the last paragraph:—

Resolved, That the several Boards herein provided may be joined, and act as one Board in the settlement of disputes between competing lines.

This was adopted without a count, and the Report, as amended, was then unanimously adopted.

Mr. Higginson moved that the time for the first meeting of the Central Board should be the Wednesday preceding the last Wednesday of January next. He proposed this day, as it was the day of meeting for the Superintendents of the several roads.

This motion was adopted.

The Report of the Committee on raising fares was then taken from the table.

Mr. Hopkinson, of the *Boston and Worcester Railroad*, said that he was here by invitation, and as there had been particular mention of the line of road with which he was connected, he felt at liberty to make some remarks. He would respectfully ask if there was an impression in the Convention that the line of which he spoke had reduced its fares so as to make such action necessary as would appear from this Report?

Judge Gove was glad to hear the question asked, and could reply, for one, that he had heard rumors of such a fact, and it was a general impression in the country that it was so. He should be glad, if wrong, to hear it contradicted.

Mr. Hopkinson then stated, that when he went into the direction of the Worcester road, there was a bargain between that and the Western road as to rates of freight. That bargain was renewed in the spring of 1849, and involved different rates for winter and summer freights, to which he acceded. There never had been any reduction whatever to meet the competition of the more Northern lines. He had consulted with Mr. Gilmore, President of the Western road, on that point, who agreed with him, that it was a matter of no consequence to their business, and therefore there was no change made to meet that competition. There was only a change made soon after from the winter to the summer rates, such as had heretofore been made every summer. He was aware that the rates had been too low on his line, and he felt warranted in saying, that they should not be sorry to let the Northern routes carry every barrel of Flour that now came over the Western and Worcester lines. What had reduced their fares was competition with water communication—the line of packets from Albany to Boston. He acceded, reluctantly, to the renewal of the arrangement, at the present rates of summer fare, for Flour; but Mr. Gilmore, who was a gentleman of great experience, said that the loss of that would carry away other business, which was of value. The lines of packets from Albany to Boston were what had really kept down the freights. It was Mr. Gilmore's theory, and seemed a reasonable one, that even if the carrying of Flour was of no profit to the Railroads, it was best to carry it, because it would otherwise keep in existence a line of packets, which would interfere with our business in other ways. This was a competition of long standing, in no way connected with the Lake Champlain competition.

Gentlemen on other roads would not probably demand that fares should be raised on the Western Railroad for the purpose of giving the business to other parties. The Northern lines were younger parties coming into the field, finding us doing a business at rates which, if not entirely satisfactory, were such as we deemed the necessities of our condition imposed upon us. It would be rather too much for them to require us to raise our rates expressly to enable them to take the business away from us. If the Western Railroad had reduced the fares to keep business from the Northern lines, which he believed was not the fact, the complaint might be just. The Western road was so situated that it would not be expedient to raise the fares; it had now a large and increasing competition between Albany and Boston, by way of Hartford, New London, Norwich, and the Harlaem Railroad, and it was doubtful how far they could, consequently, bear an increase of rate. It was his desire to act in concert with other parties having a similar interest. All the sympathies of the line which he represented were with the conservative party on this question. The great property intrusted to their charge was in the nature of a trust fund. They had no right or desire to sport with it in a race of low fares.

Mr. Edwards, of the *Cheshire Railroad*, said that this was a most important matter, and he was glad to hear the explanation of the President of the Worcester Railroad. All Railroad business should be fair and above-board. When we first took up the business at the end of the Fitchburg road, (said he,) we found that we could get the same rates which already existed, and even make some increase. We found that a remunerative rate up to the Green Mountains could be charged and collected; it is so now. On the other line, as far as Waterbury, they can do the same, for there is no competition. At Burlington, the two lines come into direct competition for the trade of that place and the country beyond. At Burlington, the rates should be the same as where we do not compete; and we could compel the two lines to this, probably, but that it does not rest with them, for there one line competes with Lake navigation. The Central road could establish higher rates better than the Rutland road, for, east of Burlington, it has no competition; but the Rutland road runs along the Lake for nearly sixty miles, and thus competes with water communication for half its way. It must, therefore, put down its rates, and so must the Central road. The Western road also increases this competition by means of this water communication, and thus indirectly helps to keep prices down. He did not suppose they had done this designedly, though it appeared that some gentlemen had thought so. But the Western Railroad prices were too low, and injured other roads, and their own also, and should therefore be raised.

The question was, whether the prices could be raised after they were once established. After establishing the plan of second-class freight, and then certain discounts, according to quantity, he did not know how far it could be dispensed with. Other roads wanted the prices put up to a remunerative rate. To be sure, the

Western Railroad had contended from the beginning with peculiar obstacles, but it was only asked now that their tariff should be regulated with an express view to avoid interference with new roads, with whom they could not successfully compete, even for business which they, the Western, had heretofore enjoyed.

Mr. Higginson wished to explain, that the Committee did not intend, in their Report, to cast any reflection on the Western Railroad. Certainly, the officers of that and of the Worcester road were not invited to this Convention to appear as culprits.

According to his view, the rates on the Western road were what, under the circumstances, they should be. But if gentlemen supposed that the present rates on the Railroad lines from Lake Champlain to Boston were rendered necessary by competition, they were mistaken, for these rates were too low—far below those necessary to meet the competition either of water communication or of the Western road.

Mr. H. then stated that the rates between Boston and Lake Champlain, by way of the Vermont Central line, were $7.50 and $5.00 per ton, and by way of the Western road and the Lake, $8.10 and $5.70 per ton; which showed the former to be the lowest, on first-class freight, by sixty cents, and on second-class freight by seventy cents. Here was the root of the whole difficulty. We all knew the through rates must be low, but, as fixed, they were unnecessarily low. This was particularly an error, when the low rate was not confined to freight from the Ogdensburg road, but was extended to that originating on Lake Champlain. This last was comparatively small; but if this was carried at the Ogdensburg rates, it must injure the local business below Burlington, by forcing upon it, also, a corresponding rate. Half of the Vermont Central freight to Boston now came from Montpelier and places this side of it, and there was no reason why the rates on this, at least, should not be raised to a highly profitable price, which, at present, they were far below.

Mr. Whittemore said it was hard for him to tell whom to call the friends of high rates. The distinction was between the friends of low rates and of lower rates, not of high and low. Directors, Presidents, the press, and, of course, the public, were all in favor of low, lower, or lowest. It was hard to say who began this, but it was clear where it would end, namely, in the ruin of Railroad business. It was time to stop; but how should we begin? The winter was a good time to begin, and a great blessing to Railroads, shutting up water communication, and giving some profits on transportation for at least a third of the year. We ought to take advantage of this. The public never complained of Railroads for charging remunerative prices, but for the underhand measures and manœuvres which were made necessary by the want of these prices.

Mr. Hopkinson said, in explanation of the plan of discounts, that they were not, on the Western Railroad, arranged by special contract with individuals, but by established rules, made before his administration, and existing on most roads.

[Judge Warren, of the *Providence Railroad*, interrupted and said, "Not on ours."

Mr. Hopkinson—"They exist on many roads. The principle originated in England. It appeared, from statistics of English roads, that with an increase of quantity and distance, the cost of transportation was very greatly reduced. Railroads could therefore afford to carry freight cheaper, when brought to them in large quantities and for great distances. A reduced rate in such cases, therefore, was reasonable."]

He had some doubts as to the duty of the Western and Worcester roads to arrange their rates with a view to other lines. But he disclaimed competition with any of these lines, though he had been erroneously reported as having threatened it. Nor was he disposed to put down fares in order to get business. He should even be disposed to condole with the Northern Railroads, if they should get all the Flour business, at Western Railroad prices.

Mr. Edwards thought that there was no necessity for lowering any rates below those of the Western Railroad, because the business of the Northern line legitimately belonged to it, and equal fares would bring all that business. He intended to say, that if the lines had made discriminating rates, in order to get business, they might discontinue them now, and let the trade find its natural channel. He had no intention of censuring the Western line.

Judge Gove said that when he alluded to the Western Railroad business, he did not know its manner of conducting business; nor did the Committee who made the Report. He was glad to learn that the rates had not been put down (as had been reported) to meet the supposed competition — a policy not only piratical, but suicidal. As to the Northern roads, he would remark, that there was so great a difference in distance between their lines and that via the Western Railroad, that they could afford to put up their prices to at least the standard of that road, and the distance saved in transportation would be at least sufficient reduction to give customers a desirable advantage.

Mr. HIGGINSON moved to amend the Report by adding as follows:—

"The Committee are also of opinion, that during the stoppage of navigation on the Lake, at least twenty per cent. should be added to the rates charged during the summer months on all freights transported by water."

This amendment was adopted without debate, and the Report was then, on motion of the same gentleman, laid upon the table.

On motion, it was then

Voted, That when the Convention adjourn, it adjourn to meet this afternoon, at four o'clock.

Voted, That the Recording Secretary of this Convention send a circular to the Presidents of the several Railroads, requesting the appointment of delegates to the Central Boards, to be organized on the Wednesday preceding the last Wednesday of January next.

The Convention then adjourned.

FOURTH DAY—AFTERNOON SESSION.

The Convention was called to order by the PRESIDENT.

GOV. PAINE, of the *Vermont Central Railroad*, announced that the Chairman of the Committee on the subject of the competition between the Rutland and

Vermont Central roads would probably be present before long, and report this afternoon.

On motion of Mr. Howe, of the *Vermont Central Railroad*, the Report on an Increase of Rates was then taken up.

Mr. Fairbanks, of the *Passumpsic Railroad*, (Mr. Howe in the chair,) said that, so far as morality was concerned, it would be right for the Railroads to get all they could. When they had established rates so high as to give the greatest revenue, even then the public would be the gainer, in consequence of the increased facilities the Railroads could grant, the time saved in transportation, the dimunition of risk, &c. If, in the adjustment of a tariff, the roads could make a given amount by the freight of one hundred tons, it would hardly be for their interest to take two hundred, even if the receipts should equal the gross amount, because the expense and labor of handling and carrying the larger quantity would reduce the net receipts, and thus they would not get paid so much. It was better, under such circumstances, to carry less in quantity, and of course incur less risk.

Among the facts elicited by the Committee, it had appeared that the fares were now less than the roads could afford; and it also appeared, that the cost of transportation on one road to Waterbury was less than to towns this side of that place. A similar state of things existed on the other road. This should not be so, and the whole tariff should be revised.

Mr. Cleveland, of the *Passumpsic Railroad*, said that Judge Follett yesterday confined his remarks to the subject of the "long" or "through" business, and its particular articles. He had understood him to say that the two roads upon Lake Champlain acted in concert in establishing the present tariff. He had examined that tariff particularly, and was of opinion that, if it were necessary to do the long or through business at these low rates, it was not necessary to do the way or local business at, or near, the same. But he did not like the tariff, for these low fares for local business affected all the other roads, more or less. He resided fifty miles from Waterbury, and about thirty-seven from St. Johnsbury; yet he could send freight to Boston from the former place for $4.80, while to send it from the latter cost $7.30. It was, therefore, very clear to him, that either the rates on the Central road were too low, or those on the Passumpsic road too high. The effect of this tariff, as at present established, must be a reduction of rates on the Passumpsic road; and if it was necessary to continue the present system, he hoped some good reason might be shown.

Mr. C. concluded by presenting the tariff of rates established on the Central Railroad, being a printed handbill, similar to that of the Rutland Railroad, already presented, which he said had been sent him, and others in the vicinity; and from the circumstance of the low rates to and from Waterbury to Boston — the twenty per cent. discount—the numeration of articles carried at these low rates all being underscored in red lines, he was led to make the inquiry, whether it was from actual necessity that these low rates were established, or whether it was done with a view to draw business on to that road that did not legitimately belong to it.

Judge Follett, of the *Rutland Railroad*, said that his road had, to a great extent, commenced operations during the present year. The tariff of fares was the result of an arrangement made by the agents of all the different roads on the two lines, which arrangement had, he thought, been faithfully carried out. Upon that basis, the Rutland road had acted. Perhaps the tariff needed revision, and the rates on some articles were too low. During the winter months, he thought the twenty per cent. discount might be suspended, as then they did not suffer from the water competition. But, as a general tariff for the whole year, he thought this was very nearly correct.

He could not agree with the suggestion that the rates of freight from Burlington to Boston ought not to be considered. One great object heretofore had been to induce people in Western Vermont to transfer their trade from New York to Boston. This had partly succeeded, and that, in some degree, from the low fares on Railroads. The trade of Western Vermont extended over an area of from seventy to eighty miles, and in order to effect the desired transfer, we must appeal to the interest of the merchants. It was a serious effort to make the change, for before the existence of the Railroads, the traders had formed all their connections in other places, had established their credits, and made their arrangements for sales and returns. It was a difficult matter to induce people to change all this, and could only be done by strong considerations of interest. He was surprised to hear that they were carrying freight at less prices than it was carried via Albany and water communication to Burlington; he had supposed the contrary. He had this day conversed with a gentleman who had informed him that he had had freight carried via Albany for $3.00

per ton, and had had freight carried over the Western Railroad at sixteen cents a hundred; but there might be some mistake on this matter, somewhere. The aim of the Rutland road had indeed been to get the trade, but not to get it at any price, pay or no pay. The Passumpsic road was doing a profitable local business, and the case alluded to by Mr. Cleveland was, he would venture to say, the only one where that road had met with a particle of competition. The case was different with roads centering at Burlington.

Mr. FAIRBANKS did not suppose that any one impeached the motives of those who arranged that tariff. As to the rate of freight to Waterbury, he remarked, that if it were based on the charges on the Passumpsic road, it would be $8.00 per ton, or more.

Gov. PAINE said that the tariff was made solely with reference to the trade with Lake Champlain. The Vermont Central Railroad had no competition with any other road, except at Burlington. He concurred in the general principles of the Report, and explained the circumstances of the Waterbury rates, which were such that they could not easily have been made otherwise.

Mr. HIGGINSON made some explanations regarding the figures he had presented during the morning debate. He maintained that Judge Follett's statement confirmed his, especially in regard to second-class freight; and it might be, that on the Western Railroad, as on many others, the established tariff was not always strictly adhered to. He was aware that there was force in the considerations presented by Judge Follett, and felt the great practical difficulty of determining the most judicious tariff.

On his motion, the Report was then again laid on the table.

Mr. Sturgis, of the *Boston and Lowell Railroad*, from the Committee on the competition between Lake Champlain and Boston, made the following

REPORT.

The Committee appointed to report to the Convention the best mode in which the Convention can consider and act upon the subject of the competition now existing between Lake Champlain and Boston, by the way of the Vermont Central and Rutland Railroads, have had the subject under careful consideration, and Report:—

That, after a full discussion, the Committee came to the conclusion, that the most effectual mode of putting an end to the competition in question, would be a division, upon equitable terms, of all the income from through freight and travel, upon both lines of road, between all points of competition; and the gentlemen representing the Vermont Central and the Rutland Railroads in the Committee, were requested to consult the Directors of their respective roads, and lay before the Committee propositions for such division.

In conformity with this request, a proposition was submitted, on the part of the Rutland Railroad, for an equal division between the two lines of the through freight and fare. On the part of the Vermont Central Railroad, it was proposed that the division should be equal for the seven summer months, and for the five winter months, the Vermont Central should receive two-thirds and the Rutland one-third. Neither of these propositions, however, proved acceptable to the other party.

As it seemed probable to the Committee that all minor points could be adjusted between the parties themselves, it was suggested, that the question of the proportion that each should receive in the division should be submitted to the decision of disinterested and competent persons, to be mutually agreed upon. This was assented to on the part of the Vermont Central Road, but declined on the part of the Rutland.

The Committee then passed the following vote — Gov. Paine and Judge Follett not voting thereon: —

Voted, That, in the opinion of this Committee, the receipts for passengers and freight, from and to all competing points, be divided equally between the Vermont Central and the Rutland and Burlington Railroads, so long as the Rutland and Burlington road takes no action in the construction of any competing line from Burlington to Swanton. And they recommend to the Directors of the several roads comprising the two lines to concur therein.

The Committee conclude by recommending the adoption of this Report, as the best mode in which the Convention can act upon the subject of the "competition now existing between Lake Champlain and Boston, by way of the Vermont Central and Rutland Railroads."

Respectfully submitted, by order of the Committee,

WILLIAM STURGIS, *Chairman.*

BOSTON, December, 1850.

Mr. STURGIS also communicated the following letter, which he had received since he left the Committee, viz.:

"BOSTON, December 13, 1850.

"To WILLIAM STURGIS, Esq., Chairman of Committee No. 2, on the competition of Railroads at Lake Champlain:

"SIR — I am authorized to signify to the Committee, that the Directors of the Rutland and Burlington

Railroad Company concur in the Resolution this day passed by said Committee, having reference to said competition.

Very respectfully,

Your obedient servant,

T. Follett,

President of the R. & B. Railroad Company."

Mr. Sturgis had but a word to say in relation to this matter. The subject had cost a great deal of labor to all the members of the Committee. The Report laid down what had been considered a fair and equitable plan of adjustment of all the difficulties. He had hoped to see these adjusted by mutual concessions. This had not yet been effected, but he did not yet despair of seeing it. His experience led him to regard it as wisest for two competing roads to aim at the best ultimate interests of both; which he believed to be best attained by an agreement securing to each certain fixed rates of fare.

Gov. Paine, of the *Vermont Central Railroad*, said that the Report was a very fair and lucid one, and had it been presented by itself, he should have remained silent. But a letter had been put in with it, which made a very different state of things. He related the history of the doings of the Committee, and said that the President of the Rutland Railroad had expressly and repeatedly stated, that he could not agree to the proviso required respecting the Swanton line of road, because his Directors had no power in relation to the matter, without consent of the stockholders, at a future meeting. This difficulty had stood in the way of an adjustment, and now, when the Committee had adjourned, after agreeing on their Report, the Rutland road came in to state (through its President) its willingness to agree. He would add no comment.

Mr. STURGIS said that when he received the letter, (after entering the hall,) he doubted what to do with it, but finally decided to present it to the Convention, as a part of the history of the case. He fully confirmed the statement of Gov. Paine, as to the course pursued by the Rutland Railroad delegates in the Committee.

Mr. FAIRBANKS, of the *Passumpsic Railroad,* moved to lay the whole subject on the table, which was carried.

Mr. FAIRBANKS then moved, and it was voted, to take up the Report on increasing the rates of fare.

Mr. FELTON, of the *Fitchburg Railroad,* said that the policy of charging a lower rate of freight on articles going through, than on articles destined for way stations, had had a bad effect on all roads, and especially on the line with which he was connected. He had often seen that roads had been obliged to reduce their rates on local freight, in consequence of such an arrangement for through freight, to a point much below a remunerative price. He also stated, that he had understood that there was a recent law in Vermont which forbade a discriminating tariff, so that the roads in that State could not now make any distinction.

Mr. FAIRBANKS explained the law, as he understood it, and said that it did not refer to "entire through freight," but only to freight from one station in the State to another.

Judge FOLLETT sustained this view. It was a law for local business, to refer only to the freight from one local station to another.

After some desultory conversation on the same subject, in which the two last speakers, and others, took part, the subject, on motion of Mr. THOMPSON, was laid on the table.

Mr. HIGGINSON suggested some arrangement as to adjournment. He thought that another Committee might be able to report by to-morrow morning, and perhaps it might be well to adjourn now, to meet at that time.

Mr. FELTON hoped that the Convention would remain together until some satisfactory result should be arrived at, though much good had been done already.

Mr. BOARDMAN, of the *Nashua and Lowell Railroad*, fully agreed with Mr. Felton.

Mr. THOMPSON, of the *Sullivan Railroad*, thought that more time was required to perfect many of the objects of the Convention. Much light had been elicited, and more would come. He accordingly moved,

"That when this Convention adjourn, it adjourn to meet on Tuesday next, at 10, A. M."

Mr. MUSSEY, of the *Passumpsic Railroad*, concurred in the views of Mr. Thompson. If the Convention should adjourn until to-morrow morning only, there was danger of hurrying the business through too fast. It would be better for all to wait until next week. The delegates represented some $100,000,000 of capital, and he thought they could afford to take, and ought to take, ample time for deliberation.

Judge FOLLETT said that, for his part, he must leave the city on Monday morning, and could not possibly be here on Tuesday next.

The PRESIDENT (Mr. FAIRBANKS) thought it important to remain together until something should be effected.

Mr. THOMPSON regretted to hear that Judge Follett was obliged to leave the city so soon, and he was willing to put off the day of the next meeting still farther, if necessary.

Mr. EDWARDS, of the *Cheshire Railroad*, said that the most important business had been reported upon, and it would, apparently, be better to remain in session another day, if one day would finish the business. If otherwise, he favored postponement.

Mr. STURGIS was not prepared to give an opinion as to the probability of an arrangement being made between the Vermont Central and Rutland roads, except such as might be gathered from his Report, read this afternoon. The Convention could judge as well as he could. The gentlemen from both those roads manifested, before the Committee, a great disposition to make some arrangement, and he was satisfied that they would find it for their interest to make one; and, indeed, absolutely necessary so to do.

Judge FOLLETT explained his reason for giving the foregoing letter to the Chairman of the Committee, as follows: — He and his friends considered that the Directors of the Rutland Railroad had no power to bind their stockholders in the matter of building the Swanton road. In the Committee, they had so stated, but the Chairman of the Committee had suggested that the representatives of the two roads (the Vermont Central and the Rutland) should give their assent to the propositions of the Committee. This he was willing to do, so far as was in the power of himself and his Directors, but the other matter was not in their power. But they had had a meeting of the Directors (or such of them as were in the city) since the Committee adjourned, and they, having understood that an expression of their opinion upon the subject would be advisable, had voted that he should send the letter which had been read. He and the Directors had no power, in the premises, to bind their stockholders; but they had authority to express their own views, and they had, in that letter, stated their willingness to abide by the decision of the Committee. It was for the stockholders to say whether they would build the road to Swanton or not.

Mr. Sturgis said that he supposed this statement to be a fact.

Mr. Higginson suggested that the Convention adjourn until a week from next Tuesday.

Mr. Thompson changed his motion, so as to read "Tuesday, December 31," which would be a fortnight from the next Tuesday; and the motion, thus amended, was agreed to.

Mr. Felton moved that the Recording Secretary be instructed to notify all the gentlemen connected with roads leading from the city, and interested in the business before the Convention, to meet at the next session.

Mr. Higginson thought that this would be placing a rather too unlimited responsibility upon the Recording Secretary.

Mr. Felton modified his resolution, and it was passed, as follows:—

Resolved, That the Secretary notify the roads now represented in this Convention, together with the Presidents, Directors and Superintendents of the Western line, the Connecticut River, Ashuelot, Champlain and St. Lawrence, and Worcester and Nashua Railroads, of the time and place for the next meeting of the Convention.

The Convention then adjourned.

FIFTH DAY.

(TUESDAY, DECEMBER 31, 1850.)

The Convention was called to order by the PRESIDENT.

The Recording Secretary read the record of the four previous meetings.

Mr. HOWE, of the *Boston and Maine Railroad*, moved, and it was

Voted, To take up the Report of the Committee on the competition between the Vermont Central and the Rutland Railroads, from Lake Champlain to Boston.

Gov. PAINE, of the *Vermont Central Railroad*, explained his views of the facts connected with the action of the Committee, and confirmed the statement formerly made by Mr. Sturgis; namely, that it was understood in Committee that the case was settled, for the present, by the declaration of the gentlemen connected with the Rutland road, that they could not act upon the proposition, except after a vote of their stockholders. The representatives of the Vermont Central road were ready to act at that time, and so stated, and were naturally surprised at the letter of Judge Follett.

Mr. Nathan Rice, of the *Rutland Railroad*, said that, though not a member of the Committee, he felt called upon (in the absence of Judge Follett) to make some explanatory remarks in behalf of the Railroad which he represented. He had understood Judge Follett to say, that he had stated to the Committee the want of power (in the Directors of the Rutland Railroad) to act *definitively* in regard to the Swanton road. But those of the Board who were in the city had afterwards met, and (in compliance with the supposed wishes of the Committee) had expressed an *opinion* in favor of the proposition. This was done in the letter of Judge Follett.

Mr. Campbell, of the *Vermont and Canada Railroad*, thought the Vermont Central Railroad would hardly accept the recommendation in the Report. They had no power to settle any thing which would shackle the Vermont and Canada road. The latter had a right to connect with the Vermont Central, or with the Rutland, or with both, and this right would not be surrendered. It was to last for eight years, and was recognized by a law passed during the last year by the Vermont Legislature. No one had a right to assume that the Vermont and Canada road would not exercise its right to lay its rails into the town of Burlington. That was a matter which concerned the Vermont and Canada road only.

Mr. Howe, of the *Boston and Maine Railroad*, said that he had supposed some progress had been made toward an agreement between the Rutland and Vermont Central Railroads. In the absence of the gentlemen who had represented the Rutland road in the Committee, he moved to lay the Report on the table.

Gov. PAINE said that the Vermont Central Railroad was ready to commit this matter to a reference, and had been so for a long time.

Mr. HOWE said it appeared that the Directors of the Rutland Railroad had no power to make such a reference; but they appeared willing to postpone it, and perhaps, if it could be postponed for a year, the case might assume a new aspect.

The motion to lay on the table was then withdrawn, by request of

Judge UPHAM, of the *Concord Railroad*, who moved a recommitment, in the hope that an amicable adjustment might yet be made.

Mr. HOWE acceded to this proposition. There had been, thus far, no unpleasant feeling exhibited in the Committee, and it might yet be able to effect something.

Mr. RICE said that there was no one more desirous than himself for a settlement of these questions, or more desirous to avoid the necessity of building the Swanton road. He had only spoken, in the absence of Judge Follett, to defend the right of building it, and show its importance to the Rutland road.

Messrs. HOWE and STURGIS thought it not desirable either to proceed in the discussion or to recommit the Report, in the absence of Judge Follett, and (after some remarks by Gov. PAINE, in explanation of his part in the discussion) the subject was *laid on the table.*

On motion of Mr. HIGGINSON, it was

Voted, That when the Report of the Committee on raising fares shall come again under discussion, each road on the main lines immediately interested therein shall be separately called on by the President to express its views, through its representatives present, upon the particular recommendations made in the Report—in such order as the President may see fit.

Voted, That this subject be made the order of the day for to-morrow, at 2, P. M., and that notice of this be given in the morning papers.

Mr. HOWE proposed for discussion, in the absence of other immediate business, the following subject:—

"The Liabilities of Railroads as Common Carriers."

Mr. HOWE said it was well known that the Boston and Maine Railroad had a deep interest in this matter. They had suffered severely by the burning of their Merchandise Station, and were involved, at the present moment, in various controversies concerning their liabilities to owners of freight, and he had taken much pains to ascertain the extent of the liability in different cases. As he understood it, the liability on *outward freight* accrues the moment it is received at the Station, whether deposited in cars, or on the floor of the house. But on *inward freight*, the liability ceases the moment the cars have arrived; after that time, the liability is not as common carriers, but as warehouse-men — only for proper care and attention. He thought the liabilities of Railroads far too great for their compensation. The public was continually demanding lower fares, and yet, as the fares went down, the liabilities seemed to increase. He hoped the subject would be fully debated, as it was very important.

The President remarked that, by the rules, this question ought to go first to the Business Committee. But, on motion of Mr. Howe, the rules were suspended, in order to take up the subject.

Mr. Hopkinson, of the *Worcester Railroad*, said that this matter of liability was a question to be settled before the Courts. If any one should go before the Legislature of either of the States for an explanatory law, he greatly feared that the burdens would be rather increased than diminished.

Mr. Howe did not expect action, but only discussion.

Mr. Sturgis thought the present generation would hardly see this question settled. Some thought that the liability ceased when goods were discharged from the cars. But if the cars arrived in the night, it was not so, as the law required that a reasonable time be allowed, in the business hours of the day, for delivery. It would doubtless be very desirable to have the Legislatures define these and other points, but he much feared that, if they undertook it, they would do the Railroads more harm than good.

Mr. Howe, in order to show that the subject was not very clear, even to legal gentlemen, quoted two opinions given by Judge Hubbard, which he thought no one present could reconcile.

Mr. Sturgis thought that gentlemen of the bar could easily reconcile them. As to notices concerning liability, if they were advertised, or if put in the cars, or if proved to be generally known, it was enough, without personally notifying each consignee.

Mr. Howe believed that the Bench had given no

attention to these general notices, when cases had been tried before the Courts. The Courts were very much in the habit of deciding according to the "fitness of things."

Mr. W. R. LEE, of the *Providence Railroad*, said that it had been decided that notice to consignees of the arrival of their goods was not necessary; that they were bound to know when the trains were due, and look after their goods. It had been ruled, that if notice of a limit as to time, or other liability as common carriers, could be brought home decidedly to a consignee, then it would hold. As to liability after the arrival of goods, there was a difference between Railroads and common teamsters, the former being warehouse-men as well as carriers, creating liabilities different in kind and degree. He thought that gentlemen would get all the information they needed on this subject, by reading or referring to Angell on the Law of Common Carriers. He thought it a doubtful experiment to appeal to legislation, but each road might select particular cases, and test them in Court.

Mr. HOWE said that his road was now doing this, in several cases.

Mr. STURGIS said that this was a good plan, if we looked only to the public good. But if the good of the corporation was to be consulted, he thought it would prove most profitable to pay.

Mr. HOPKINSON thought that these matters generally found their way into the Legislature, through the medium of individuals who had quarrelled with some Railroad about some private claim, and on being chosen to the Legislature, brought the subject up as soon as possible.

Mr. Higginson thought it very important to have the different questions of liability settled, but thought this could best be done by the Courts. The Supreme Court had already settled many such questions; as, for instance, in a late case on the Worcester Railroad, where it was decided that one employé, injured through the fault of another, could not recover against the corporation. If any one should now go to a lawyer with a similar case, this decision would be at once referred to, as rendering it impossible for a suit to be maintained. But no legislation could be thus decisive.

Mr. Nesmith was satisfied that Railroads would have a better chance in New Hampshire Courts, than in the New Hampshire Legislature. He also thought that Railroads were not sufficiently compensated for the risks run by them.

Some farther desultory conversation took place, after which, on motion of Mr. Rice, it was

Voted, That when this Convention adjourn, it adjourn until to-morrow, at 10, A. M.

The Convention then adjourned.

SIXTH DAY.

(WEDNESDAY, JANUARY 1, 1851.)

The Convention was called to order by the President. The Journal of yesterday was read and approved.

On motion of Mr. Howe, of the *Boston and Maine*

Railroad, the question assigned for this morning was laid on the table.

On motion of Mr. Howe, the Report of the Committee on the competition between Lake Champlain and Boston was taken up, and, without debate, *recommitted* to the original Committee.

On motion of Judge Follett, Mr. Linsley, of the Rutland road, was added to the Committee.

On motion of Mr. Higginson, the special order of the day was taken up—being the Report on Raising the Rates of Fare.

The President, in pursuance of the order adopted yesterday, then called on the *Fitchburg* Road, and there was no response.

Then on the *Lowell* Road, with the same result.

The President then called on the *Boston and Maine* Road.

Mr. Howe said that this road was rather peculiarly situated in respect to this particular question. It was connected with a line extending Eastward, and rates of freight were established, in connection with other roads, which it would probably be difficult, at present, to alter. They now contemplated extending an arm to the North. They desire to be consistent in all matters. It would be awkward to have different rates on different portions of their road, extending in different directions; but they should want to do as others did in respect to prices.

The *Rutland* Road being next called on, Judge Follett referred to what he had said on the subject at former meetings. One portion of the subject had been voted on in the Convention—the discount on second-class freight—and had been immediately acted on by the two roads leading from Lake Champlain, before the delegates left the city. Both roads now charged the rates established by their common Tariff, without deduction. He could not say how long the present rates would last, but probably at least through the winter. Second-class freight was now $6.00; formerly, it was $6.00, minus the deduction. The Convention had also fixed a rate for cattle-trains, and the two roads had since come to an arrangement on this matter, both charging $40.

Another evil used to exist—the carting, at Burlington, of both freight and passengers to and from the Railroads. This, also, had been discontinued, and he hoped permanently. He thought no increase of rates upon his line desirable. Their difficulties were greater than gentlemen were aware of. For eight months in the year, they were in competition with water communication and the Western Railroad. New York must enter into their consideration. Burlington people had a habit of boating their freight to Troy, and there deciding between Boston and New York. Bills of lading were often filled out with instructions to this effect. Iron had been carried from Boston to Vermont, last year, at $3.25 per ton, as Gov. Paine had said. Such cases often occurred, and these facts could not be disregarded.

As to passengers, the fare to Burlington was $6.00; and the stages had carried passengers at the same price—not very often, but sometimes; but now there were no stages. The roads below had their share of this price. The usual rate on the Rutland road was three cents a mile, but on through passengers to Boston, the upper roads did not get so much. He was inclined to think, that if less than $6.00 were to be charged to Lake Champlain, it would be of great advantage, especially during the summer travel. The fare by steamboat was lower than this, and likely to be lower yet. An agent of the Steamboat Company had told him that, next summer, the rate from Burlington to New York would be put at $3.00. He was inclined to think that the roads would hardly bear higher rates.

He did not know why the Committee's recommendation of low prices for freight from Ogdensburg would not apply also to other through freight from Burlington, or the new trade from other places. Many articles that could be sent to market, especially to Boston, by the Rutland road, were rough and bulky, and required no great capital to get them ready for market. High freights would increase their cost more than 100 per cent., and that would be more than they would sell for, on arrival. Iron, he believed, was now carried for 50 per cent. more than the same could be transported by water. He would not go below a remunerative price, for that or any other article, but we could not go higher; and here he disagreed with the Report.

Mr. LINSLEY, of the *Rutland* Road, did not understand what was meant in the Report by "the addition of 20 per cent. during the stoppage of navigation." If this referred merely to second-class freight, the object had been already accomplished, as stated by Judge Follett; if to all freight, he did not suppose it would be very objectionable. He did not know why there should be a reduction on Ogdensburg freight, except for the sake of getting the freight—the same principle for which the Rutland road had contended. As to the

New York business not being considered, perhaps that was, at this time, of little consequence.

Judge FOLLETT believed that he had said that they had had regard to New York business in making their Tariff. All the great Boston roads had aimed to divert business thither from other places. Both roads (the Rutland and Vermont Central) had united in forming the present Tariff. It was not true, that the upper roads had forced injurious rates of freight on the lower ones. The Tariff adopted at Burlington was formed in Boston, by all the different Superintendents, and while he was opposed to raising it, he yet was not willing to claim its whole paternity. As for underbidding, he knew nothing of it; both roads, he believed, followed the Tariff they had agreed upon.

Mr. LINSLEY spoke of the article of Flour. By the spirit of this Report, though Flour went from Burlington, some to Boston and some to New York, we must not take it, to prevent it all from going to the latter city, even if we can make a thousand dollars by it, because we must not interfere with the New York trade. So, the article of Marble might be wanted at Savannah, and the freight be less from Boston than from New York; according to the Report, we must not take it to Boston at a low rate, to compete with the New York trade. This he thought poor policy.

Mr. CONANT, of the *Rutland* Road, approved the removal of the twenty per cent. discount, but only on some articles. Marble, for instance, car-wheels, manufactured in the country, and fire-bricks, were articles which must be carried cheaply, or not at all. Certain goods—perishable articles, for instance, as fruits, and (in summer) butter and cheese—would pay higher rates. But on all the great business, which must be fostered, the fares should be low enough to obtain it.

Mr. Derby, of the *Fitchburg* Road, agreed with the gentlemen of the Rutland Road, both in regard to low fares and to the New York competition. The Western Railroad had already diverted much New York business, and more should be diverted. There was much freight intended for Maine and the British Provinces which might as well go through Boston as New York. Flour was eight or ten cents a barrel higher, generally, in Boston, than in New York, and we ought to get the freight of it. Unless Boston was to be a mere appendage to New York, we must have low freights on Western produce. Then Boston might one day speak of its millions of tons of freight, as New York did in speaking of the Erie Canal.

The Report said we should not carry freight at less than cost, but it did not say what cost was. That cost depended on the average load taken by an engine, and was less for a wholesale than for a retail traffic, and he would therefore charge more for the local trade than for the through traffic with the Lakes. On the Reading Railroad, freight was carried at a cost of less than two-thirds of a cent per ton a mile. On this line, the ascending trains were empty, and the average load did not exceed one hundred and eighty tons. On the Fitchburg Railroad, the through-freight trains were, on an average, about equal to those on the Reading, and if the Vermont roads would maintain the same average, the cost between Boston and Lake Champlain would fall below $2.50 per ton. If we could carry this Western freight for $3.50 and $6.00 per ton, and make a profit on it, however small, he approved it.

He should not approve of $2.00 per ton, if we were to lose by it. He should be sorry to have the Convention adopt the principle of the Report, that we were not to keep in view the New York competition.

He referred to a time in the early days of the Worcester Railroad, when the down freight only averaged twelve tons to a train, and it was proposed among the Directors to farm out the whole by contract, at $15,000 a year, for a term of years. That road had since been doing a freight business worth more than $200,000 a year, and he believed the Western business was now worth at least $700,000. He feared lest, in their anxiety for local business, gentlemen would forget how much was yet to be obtained from Canada, Michigan, and the far West.

He could partially accept the proposition of the Report in regard to winter rates. He would take the freight-tariff, as established between Albany and Boston, consider the difference in grades and distances, and apportion the rates accordingly. If the Western road, costing so much as it did, could divide seven or eight per cent., why should not we on the Northern lines, under more favorable circumstances, do the same? He would strive for this, to keep the through Tariff low, (except on some few expensive or perishable articles,) and compete with the Erie Canal for the great trade of the West.

Mr. Chapman, of the *Vermont and Massachusetts* Road, expressed a doubt whether there was any distinct issue presented in the Report.

Mr. Hopkinson could not agree with the Report, that there should be no regard paid to water competition. Railroads were artificial channels, intended to compete with natural ones, and should put their prices low enough to effect this. Prices must, of course, be discriminating; but it might often be desirable to carry some articles at small profit, or even at a loss, for the sake of securing and fostering the business. He instanced Marble and Flour. On the latter, there was direct competition with water communication. Flour was rather a desirable freight, being clean, easily handled, and in large quantities, and perhaps, taking the whole line into view, it gave a small profit; at any rate, they thought it best to take it, for considerations before given. They would be glad to raise any of their prices, if practicable. A regular tariff of three cents a mile for passengers would not, under some circumstances, diminish travel. The present rates on the Worcester road were two and a half cents, and the Western road, three cents; but the through fares were less.

The *Cheshire* Road being next called on, Mr. Edwards said that his views in regard to New York competition had been somewhat modified, and he now believed it necessary to take it into view. He could approve no absolute rule, unless it were to take nothing except at a remunerative price, however small. There was no danger of the other extreme — competition would take care of that. But reductions and discounts had been carried too far. The Northern roads were not to blame for this; it had been all experimental so far, and nothing permanently fixed.

The *Vermont and Massachusetts* Road being called on, Mr. Chapman again objected to the Report, as contradictory in regard to water competition, and vague in regard to remunerative prices.

The *Northern* Road being called on, Mr. Stearns

explained that it was thought best by the Committee not to have any particular reference to the business of New York, and not to go below the prices of the Western Railroad. He moved that the subject be continued to-morrow.

Mr. Fairbanks moved, and it was voted, that when the Convention adjourn, it adjourn until 10, A. M., to-morrow.

Some desultory conversation then occurred upon the laws of Vermont, and Judge Follett explained that the law which forbade the discrimination in rates for freight had reference alone to local freight, and not to that to or from Burlington.

The Convention then adjourned.

SEVENTH DAY.

(THURSDAY, JANUARY 2, 1851.)

The Convention was called to order by the President. The Journal of yesterday was read and approved.

The subject announced for discussion was the Report on Raising the Rates of Fare.

Mr. Higginson said that, as a member of the Committee, he should, at a proper time, propose to amend the Report. It proposed to confine attention to such freight as was to be conveyed by some mode between

Lake Champlain and Boston; and it opposed the policy of attempting to increase this amount by diversions from New York, if this was to be secured at rates excessively low.

It had been estimated, that by the present rates on some through freight, but eighty cents per ton had been received, by one of the upper Railroads, for carrying freight one hundred miles, and furnishing cars for one hundred and fifty more. As to the Passumpsic road, there was a difference; the rates were higher on that road than on the two great roads from Lake Champlain, but not by any means too high, as he thought Mr. Derby himself, were he present, would admit. The prices on the latter roads were now much too low, and affected the others, at Concord, Manchester and Lowell, as well as Boston. The greater part of the Northern freight stopped short of Lowell; and he referred to a statistical statement to show that the reduction on freight was enormous; that the upper Railroads had injured themselves and others in fostering a through business, at the expense of their local traffic. If the freight was reduced to one point, it must be to another, and so on. The Committee thought that, under these circumstances, the New York trade, below a certain point, which caused all this reduction, should be thrown out of account. Let the point at which these low fares may commence be situated, like Rouse's Point, so as not to affect the local rates below it, and then let them be confined to the through freight to Boston. Franklin County, in Vermont, should be made a source of profit, as well as Caledonia County. He suggested an amendment, (which was supported by Judge Gove,) but after some conversation as to points of order, moved a recommitment of the Report, which was accordingly voted.

After a brief consultation, Judge Gove, on the part of the Committee, reported it back, with the following amendment:—

"After the words 'Albany and Boston,' in the first sentence of the Report, (p. 50,) insert the words, 'and to the through communication, by water, from Burlington to Boston.'"

Judge Gove said, there was a point beyond which low fares could not be carried. He could not judge of the Lake Champlain roads, but harm was being done to the whole community by reducing fares below remunerative rates, and accustoming people to regard Railroads as built to work for nothing. It was difficult, also, to discriminate as to distance. People were suspicious if they saw freight carried cheaper the farther it went. Rates were too low, every where, however. Eighty cents would not pay for cars; and it would be good economy to hire cars, at that rate, and lay up the others. From calculations made from authentic sources, he found that the Lowell road received 7,000 tons of freight from Vermont, over the Central road, last year, while, over the Nashua road, more than 9,000 tons were brought from the Central road; which showed that 2,000 tons did not go through. He read a statement showing the operation of the business, and showing that the through business, at cheap rates, had not been beneficial to the lower roads. His opinion was decided, that the rates were too low, and should be raised.

Mr. FAIRBANKS thought that there was no difficulty in the theory of the matter; it was only that the classification of the Tariff was not complete; some articles should be higher than at present. To this, he and his Directors would probably agree. There should be a revision. Some articles were carried for less than the cost of insurance. It was said that lately an amount of property, valued at more than $35,000, was carried over the Vermont Central Railroad for $4.50! This was an extreme case, but this should not happen. He thought that freight on dry goods and on hazardous goods might be increased considerably, without complaint.

Gentlemen of the Rutland road thought it important to foster new branches of business, as in the case of Marble, and they should judge for themselves about it. Mr. Hopkinson thought it desirable to aim at large quantities; and here, also, roads should judge for themselves, as in the case of Flour, or of Fire-Brick, Pig Iron, Marble, &c. But it was a pity, for the sake of these long through-trains, to sacrifice the local freight, which had made the short roads profitable before the extensions were built, and might still do so. It was dangerous to interfere with the dividends of these roads; they were built for the sake of dividends, and, if these were not obtained, we should one day be called to account for it. But there should be a careful revision of tariffs, and he favored the appointment of a Committee, who should thoroughly investigate this subject, and be, if necessary, paid for it.

Mr. HIGGINSON suggested that the proposed Committee would be useless, until some general statement of principles was assented to.

The *Concord* Road being then called on, Judge Upham expressed his approval of the Report, so far as he had considered it. Its object appeared to be the assertion of certain general principles, the basis of which was the assumption that the present rates were too low. The Committee appeared to think that no competition should be regarded, except the rates of freight from Burlington through to Boston, by water or by land. We could not undertake to take care of the interests of Boston, but only of those of the Railroads. So far as he knew, every thing went well, so long as the roads only extended to the Green Mountains, and the Vermont Central road was open only to Montpelier. The lower roads were better off until then; but when the line was extended to the Lake shore, it at once came in competition with water communication. But he thought that the Boston business could be made a paying business; while, if New York could do any business cheaper than Boston, that business naturally belonged to New York, and it was not our affair to prevent its going there.

The through business from Ogdensburg was different in its nature from any other, and New York would not compete for it. We should there charge remunerative prices, though those could be lower than on local freight, in view of the quantity. The through rates need not affect the local rates, and then there would be no difficulty. He wished that the Committee had gone farther, and said that this should be a Boston business, and not a business for the whole Atlantic coast. He wished the principle they laid down to include the understanding that there should be a conference among all the roads on the lines concerning the rates, so as to secure uniformity and equitable distribution. Should the idea of New York business be abandoned, he thought all might be satisfied.

The *Sullivan* Road being called on, Mr. Thompson said that he spoke with some diffidence, from having so recently come into the Direction, but he thought the present rates too low. There was no doubt, now, of the general success of Railroads, and we were bound to look to the interests of stockholders. The lower roads were the head and limbs of the great trunks, and he thought the principle good of looking first to the business naturally belonging to Boston. If other business could be brought in, very well; but he agreed with the Report, that we should not take into view the water communication to New York.

Judge Follett, of the *Rutland* Road, wished to explain that the Tariff of that road had caused no complaint to the Vermont Central road, or to the lower roads, except in some few particulars. There was an objection to the twenty per cent. discount, which had now been removed.

Mr. Stearns, of the *Northern* Road, said that he understood that the freight charged on the Rutland line, from the Lake to Boston, left only sixty-four cents to be divided between the Cheshire, Vermont and Massachusetts, and Fitchburg roads.

Judge Follett said the price was $6.00 to Boston, and the lower roads all received their proportion of $2.94.

Judge Upham said that, on the Concord line, no change had been made since the original arrangement, and the lower roads were now called on to make a reduction. As for the Concord road, that always settled with all other roads alike.

On motion of Judge GOVE, the Convention voted to adjourn, to meet at the room of the Railroad Superintendents, No. 11½ Tremont Row, at 3½, P. M.

SEVENTH DAY—AFTERNOON SESSION.

The Convention was called to order by the PRESIDENT, and after some conversation on points of order, the subject of yesterday was resumed.

Mr. LINSLEY, of the *Rutland* Road, thought it important to ascertain on what ground we were proceeding. He disagreed with the Report in regard to New York competition. One important object of all these Railroads was to secure all business, so far as possible, to Boston. Hence, Boston capital was invested in them. This object might often require low fares, and even rates not remunerative, as in the case of the Western Railroad. But he thought the whole matter might most safely be left to the roads themselves.

Mr. HIGGINSON believed that some of the rates between Burlington and Boston were not remunerative. The Western road was not a case in point, for that road took Flour only in large quantities at the low rates. The last speaker had not fully considered the point conceded by the Committee as to the Ogdensburg business. The principle of the Report was not new; the Western road had never thought of putting down fares for the sake of bringing New York business to Boston; and Boston, moreover, having invested largely in these roads, was interested in obtaining remunerative prices.

Mr. Derby feared that gentlemen were disposed to forget that the interest of Boston in obtaining the great business of the West was coincident with that of the Railroads. We could not afford to risk the loss of the Lake Champlain trade. Every loss of freight to the roads was a loss to Boston, and our roads prospered with the growth of Boston. Trade had much changed since Railroads were built. Within the last half year, people from Manchester and Concord, who used to come to Boston, had been able to go to Ogdensburg for flour and grain. Much of the local business had left the roads near Boston, and we must now encourage the through trade.

He spoke of the trade from Lake Champlain to Boston. He understood that the lowest charge from Burlington to Boston was $4.80, after deducting the twenty per cent. discount. The freight from Burlington to New York was $2.70, and from New York to Boston $1.30—making the through freight that way $4.00. Our roads made a new business, through a new channel, and he thought we should find it a valuable one; but it could only be secured by fares low enough to compete with the water route by New York. While the canals were closed, the twenty per cent. discount might be removed; and he also concurred in the proposition to change many articles from second to first-class freight. He thought butter, cheese and oats might be raised. But he could not concur in the general principles of the Report. On the English roads, the average rate for passengers was two to three cents per mile; and yet these roads cost as many pounds sterling as ours cost dollars.

Mr. Linsley did not see why the Report should make a distinction between freight over the Rutland road from Lake Champlain, and that from the Ogdensburg road. It gave a great advantage to the rival road. The Rutland road meant to do something in making business for Boston, and Boston should do something for it.

Mr. Higginson explained, that the Committee only aimed to lay down general principles, and had no intention of benefitting any other road, at the expense of the Rutland road. Mr. Felton, who drew the Report, could not, of course, be suspected of such an intention.

Mr. Chapman, from the *Vermont and Massachusetts* Road, inquired why, if the Ogdensburg freight should be transported, in large quantities, at a reduced price, the same amount of freight should not be transported on the same low terms from Lake Champlain?

Mr. Higginson replied, that the rule was not extended to freight originating on Lake Champlain, because this, it was supposed, would be much smaller in quantity than Western freight, and because any rate applied to it would be more likely to extend to the local freight below it.

Judge Follett said that there was a great amount of freight centering at Burlington, which did not come from Ogdensburg, but by water, from different places. Much came by British vessels; and, moreover, the Lake was always open at Burlington some weeks later than it was below, and freight could come there long after it was shut out of the canals. Why, then, grant favors to the Ogdensburg freight at the expense of this? He proposed to take this freight at a price they could afford. They were bound by the present Tariff to take it at $4.80. He thought they ought to take it at $4.00; and if they had been allowed to take it at this rate, they could have carried a large amount which they had now lost.

Mr. FAIRBANKS, of the *Passumpsic* Road, said that, in the adjustment of the Tariff, there were undoubtedly errors. There should be some considerations of expediency in regard to Flour and Iron;—of the latter, he thought that no great quantity ever was or would be brought from Lake Champlain. He had never found iron any cheaper in Burlington than in Boston.

Judge FOLLETT thought the state of trade in Boston was chiefly to be considered. In fixing the Tariff, one aim had been to induce the people of Vermont to come to Boston with their business, for which low fares were necessary. It was said, in the country, that Boston was the best market for West India goods, and the merchants of Canada brought their goods through Lake Champlain. West India goods and teas were now purchased, for Canada and Western Vermont, in the New York market, because transportation was cheaper than from Boston. The Railroad had not yet had the effect desired, in this respect. One inducement calculated on was the carrying produce to Boston, and getting return freights, in merchandise, to supply the country, not only with groceries, but manufactured goods. If this could be effected, the business would be good. As it was, he knew of no article named in the Tariff which did not pay a remunerative price.

Judge UPHAM, of the *Concord* Road, said that he understood the Committee to desire that every article should pay as high a price as the cost of carrying it. It was not expected that, if the rate between Burlington and New York city was $2.70, freight should be carried at that price between Burlington and Boston, because the roads could not afford it. Trade must always find its own channel, and that was always the cheapest. The principle of the Report was, that rates should be as cheap as could be afforded, and no cheaper. The details must be decided hereafter. The real question was on the principle.

Mr. DERBY thought that, after all, the speakers did not differ so widely as might have been supposed. He then spoke of his own experience in freighting iron on other roads, and said that he had lately contracted for a large lot of lumber, which he would have willingly bought on Lake Champlain, and transported over the Northern roads, but was obliged to go elsewhere, from the high price of freight. From this, he inferred that the public might reason in the same way.

Judge FOLLETT asked to hear it explained why the Rutland Road could not have the advantage of all the trade it could do? The Vermont Central Road now got the Ogdensburg business, and the Rutland did not.

Mr. CHAPMAN hoped the Report would be amended on this point, as he could not otherwise vote for it.

Judge UPHAM thought the Report simply stated a principle, and had no disguised meaning. He did not understand that any difference was designed between the freight from Ogdensburg to Boston, and that from Lake Champlain, or Burlington, to Boston. We were expected to fix the rates of freight so as to secure the Boston business, and not let it go over any other road, so long as we could get it at prices as low as could be afforded. He never supposed that, in advocating this Report, he was advocating any partial legislation.

Mr. HIGGINSON read extracts from the Report, showing that the Rutland Road was considered, and that no advantage was intended to be given to any other road, in opposition to it. The rule laid down in the Report applied to Western freight generally, whether coming to Lake Champlain by the Ogdensburg Railroad, or by water, and thus included that received by the Rutland Railroad.

Judge Follett spoke of a large quantity of wheat which was imported into Burlington, last year, from Michigan, and asked why a miller, buying wheat in Burlington, and manufacturing it into flour, should not have as good an opportunity of sending it to Boston, as those who manufactured it elsewhere, and sent it over the Ogdensburg Road?

Mr. Chapman, of the *Vermont and Massachusetts* Road, did not see why freight, coming in large quantities over the Ogdensburg Road, should be considered of more advantage to the trade, and deserving of more consideration, than that which came in large quantities, from other sources, through Burlington.

Judge Upham thought that there would be some reason in this observation, but that the premises were incorrect, and there was no such distinction.

Mr. Higginson agreed with Judge Upham, but thought that if the phraseology of the Report could be made clearer by recommitment, it would be very desirable. The object of the Committee was to secure the trade of the West, and, at the same time, to prevent any injury to the local traffic of the roads on both the great lines.

Mr. Mussey, of the *Passumpsic* Road, then moved, and it was voted, to recommit the Report.

The following votes were then passed:

Voted, That when the Convention adjourn, it adjourn to meet at the same place to-morrow, at 12, M.

Voted, That the Recording Secretary give notice to the first and third Committees to meet at this place at 9, A. M., and that he give notice, in the morning papers, of the place and hour of meeting of the Convention, and the subject for discussion.

Voted, That Mr. BOARDMAN be appointed to serve on the Committee on the subject of the competition existing between the White River Junction and Boston, in place of Mr. BOWERS, in case the latter gentleman should not be present at the morning meeting; and,

That Mr. LINSLEY be appointed to serve on the Committee on raising fares, in place of Mr. BRADLEY, in the same contingency.

The Convention then adjourned.

EIGHTH DAY.

(FRIDAY, JANUARY 3, 1851.)

The Convention was called to order by the PRESIDENT. The Journal of yesterday was read and approved.

Judge GOVE, of the first and third Committees, made the following joint

REPORT.

To the Convention of Railroad Directors and Superintendents of the Northern and Western lines, now assembled at Boston:

The Committee to whom was referred the subject of rates for Passengers and Freight, respectfully report:

They would, in the first place, recommend, generally, that in no case should so low a rate be adopted as to leave a doubt of its affording some direct profit.

In the second place, they would recommend a general principle in regard to rates for freight between Boston and Lake Champlain:—That these should be adjusted with reference only to the business naturally going between these points, and without any view of diverting freight to Boston which would naturally go to New York; and that they should, therefore, be governed by the rates of other lines only so far as these present other modes of communication to and from Boston; and that they should in no degree be affected by the cost of transportation to and from New York.

There are represented in the Convention two great direct Northern Railroad lines between Lake Champlain and Boston. These have necessarily to compete for the through freight with two indirect Southern lines; the one, by water communication all the way to Boston; the other, by water to Albany and Troy, and thence, by the Western and Worcester Railroads, to Boston. But the Northern routes, composed completely of Railroads, have the advantage over either of the other modes, in time and certainty; and they should avail themselves of their advantage, by charging an enhanced price.

Thus, if, by the Western Railroad route, the charge for through transportation be $6.00 a ton, then something more than $6.00 a ton may be charged by either of the direct Railroad lines; and a yet larger difference may be made in favor of the latter, as compared with the entire water route. But, if the rate between Lake Champlain and New York be $3.00, this, in the opinion of your Committee, constitutes no reason why that on the Railroad lines between Lake Champlain and Boston should be reduced at all.

The Committee think it may possibly be desirable to waive this rule during the close of navigation in the winter, and to make an exception in favor of bonded goods going from Boston to Canada. But they are aware of no other case in which it cannot wisely be applied.

In making these recommendations in regard to Lake Champlain freight, the Committee are influenced mainly by the belief that a lower rate is now established for that freight than is justified by the principle laid down, and by the fact that the very low rates established for through-freight have necessarily depressed those upon way-freight, and that this evil is extending in a manner to justify serious apprehensions of detriment to all the roads concerned. The Committee, therefore, submit the following resolutions.

CHARLES F. GOVE, *for the Committee.*

Resolved, That in no case should so low a rate for freight be adopted, as to leave a doubt as to its affording some direct profit.

Resolved, That the following general principles should be adopted in regard to the rates for freight between Boston and Lake Champlain:—That these should be adjusted with reference only to the business naturally going between these points, and without any view of diverting freight to Boston which would* naturally go to New York; and that they should, therefore, be governed by the rates of other lines, only so far as these present other modes of communication to and from Boston; and that they should in no degree be affected by the cost of transportation to and from New York, only.

On motion of Judge GOVE, this Report was accepted.

On the question of adopting the Resolutions ap-

* See amendment beyond.

pended to the Report, a division was called for, (by Mr. POTTER, of the *Contoocook* Road,) and it was voted that each should be considered separately.

Mr. HALE, of the *Cheshire* Road, advocated the first Resolution.

Mr. HIGGINSON called for the yeas and nays, which were ordered.

Judge GOVE said he could vote cordially for the first Resolution, as the only one which could be adopted with any justice to stockholders.

Judge FOLLETT had not intended to debate the merits of the Report, nor should he now, had not the yeas and nays been ordered. This first Resolution was a new proposition. The word "profit" had been substituted for the word "remunerative," in the first Report, and presented a new meaning. He must suggest the leaving this matter to the several Railroads, who might occasionally think it best to do certain business without *immediate* profit.

Mr. STURGIS inquired whether the Resolutions were understood to be obligatory or only recommendatory?

Mr. HOWE, of the *Boston and Maine Railroad*, replied that they were only recommendatory.

Judge FOLLETT said that if such were the case, he had no objection.

Mr. HOWE said that he spoke only for himself, and not for the Convention.

Mr. WHITTEMORE supposed the Resolution was only recommendatory, and would have weight chiefly as expressing a sort of Railroad public sentiment. It was good, as recognizing the fact that Railroads had a *right* to some profit, which seemed sometimes forgotten. He admitted that there might be cases where temporary loss on freight might bring ultimate profit, but these came within the spirit of the Resolution.

Mr. Fairbanks thought the Resolution only asserted a general principle, and could not bind any one road. Still, if it should pass unanimously, he should consider each road that voted for it as agreeing to adhere to it, except in extreme cases.

Judge Follett approved the principle of the Resolution, but thought its terms too exclusive; he would prefer to strike out the words "in no case."

Mr. Sturgis would not oppose the amendment, but thought the general principle a very important one. He should be glad to see it incorporated by law in every Railroad charter. He did not like the principle of the Western Railroad Flour business, before referred to.

Mr. Hopkinson, of the *Worcester* Road, explained. He had said that there was "some doubt" as to any profit from this business on the Western Railroad; but he had also expressed his opinion that there was a small actual profit to the Western Road.

Mr. Sturgis moved to amend the Resolution according to Judge Follett's suggestion, so that it might read—

"That there should not be adopted so low a rate for freight as to leave a doubt of its affording some direct profit."

This amendment was adopted, and on motion of Mr. Linsley, the vote ordering the yeas and nays was reconsidered. The Resolution, as amended, was then unanimously adopted.

The next question being on the adoption of the second Resolution,

Mr. Linsley inquired why we should not take into consideration the trade with New York? The Resolution said, "the business *naturally* going between these points," &c. That embraced the whole trade. Man has made artificial modes of transportation to interfere with natural ones. Suppose the passenger fare to New York to be $5.00 and to Boston $7.00, why were we not to consider these facts, and reduce our rates to secure this travel? The question was, whether we could take these different kinds of business and make a profit, by lowering the rates according to circumstances.

Mr. Sturgis thought the last speaker was under some misunderstanding. He understood the whole proceeding as referring to the arrangement of a general Tariff between Burlington and Boston.

Mr. Fairbanks wished gentlemen to remember that they were not legislating for particular cases, but fixing general principles. Every thing should be considered. An immediate profit of 100 per cent. might involve an ultimate loss of $1000. Admitting the force of Mr. Linsley's suggestion about passengers, he would ask if a reduction of fares from Burlington, to meet New York competition, might not lead to the loss of thousands of dollars on the great mass of passengers? As to Lumber, which had been referred to, he had yet to learn that it ever had been brought from Lake Champlain to Boston.

Judge Follett said that large quantities of Lumber were carried on the Rutland road, and it was to be had in plenty all along the coast.

Mr. Fairbanks admitted it, but had never heard of its going to Boston.

Mr. Derby could not vote for the Resolution, as it stood. Naturally, no freight came from Lake Champlain to Boston, but all went to New York. We had made artificial channels to bring it to Boston, and ought to use them. He was surprised to hear Judge Gove's remark that only about 9000 tons were brought last year over the Vermont Central Railroad to his road. He knew of one gentleman who would have furnished more business than that at $4.00 a ton. He was one of those who believed that a great trade was open to us from Montreal, which would come over the St. John's road, now in process of building. He would, in the matter of a Tariff, when competing with a water route, take into view the cost of insurance, the certainty, the risk, and the saving of time, would add for these to the cost by water, and would not carry freight at so low a rate as not to afford a profit. In arranging such Tariff, it was indispensable to refer to the New York business. As to the local business, he would discriminate; he would get for it as high a price as it would afford. The freight from Albany to Springfield, on the Western Railroad, was now higher than that from Albany to Boston. We might, in many cases, command good prices for our local traffic; but it is subject, at certain points, to competition.

There are many new routes built, or in progress, to connect the inland lines with the sea, at Portland, Portsmouth, Salem, New London and Hartford, which would divert the business from Boston, in case of an excess in charges. All this required caution and discrimination.

On motion, the Convention adjourned to 3½, P. M.

EIGHTH DAY—AFTERNOON SESSION.

The Convention was called to order by the PRESIDENT.

On motion of Judge GOVE, the subject first in order (which was the unfinished business of the morning) was laid on the table.

Judge GOVE then offered the following Resolution, at the suggestion of Judge Upham, who was necessarily absent:—

Resolved, That a Committee of two persons from each of the lines between Boston and Burlington, via Fitchburg, Cheshire, and Rutland Railroads, and Lowell, Northern, and Vermont Central Railroads, be appointed by each of these lines — to be joined by one from the Passumpsic, one from the Sullivan, and one from the Boston and Maine Railroads — to agree upon and establish rates of freight between Boston and Burlington, whether Western or local freight; and, in connection with the Committee appointed by the Ogdensburg Railroad, to establish rates of freight between Ogdensburg and Boston.*

Mr. HIGGINSON said he did not understand that Judge Upham expected that this Committee should act decisively. The upper roads had usually made the Tariffs for themselves, and the lower ones had agreed to the arrangement. This Resolution was only offered, as he understood, to provide for obtaining a concurrence of the lower roads before any Tariff should be decided upon, instead of afterwards, as had heretofore been the custom.

* See page 122 for an amended form of this Resolution, as it finally passed.

On motion of Wm. Sturgis, Esq., the Resolution was laid on the table.

Mr. Sturgis, of the *Lowell Railroad*, then made the following

REPORT.

The Committee to whom was re-committed the subject of the competition now existing between Lake Champlain and Boston, by the way of the Vermont Central and the Rutland Railroads, report:

That after farther discussion and consideration, separate communications, in writing, were made to the Committee by the President of the Vermont Central and the President of the Burlington and Rutland Railroads, which communications are now submitted to the Convention, as forming a part of this Report; and the Committee ask to be discharged from the farther consideration of the subject.

Per order of the Committee,

William Sturgis, *Chairman.*

Boston, January 3, 1851.

[copy.]

Boston, January 3, 1851.

Wm. Sturgis, Esq., Chairman of the Committee of Convention:

Sir,—I am directed by the Committee from the Vermont Central Railroad Company to inform you, and through you, the Committee of the Convention, that they cannot accept of the proposition or recommendation contained in the Resolution reported by you to the Convention, to wit:—

"That, in the opinion of this Committee, the receipts for passengers and freight from and to all competing points, be divided equally between the Vermont Central and the Rutland and Burlington Railroads, *so long* as the Rutland and Burlington road takes no action in the construction of any competing line from Burlington to Swanton; and they recommend to the Directors of the several roads comprising the two lines to concur therein": —

Because the proposition or recommendation contained in the foregoing Resolution is not fair and just to the Vermont Central, inasmuch as the Rutland and Burlington Railroad Company have the power to prolong for ever the arrangement proposed, or to terminate it the next day after made, and the Central have no power over the arrangement, when made.

I am farther instructed by the Committee to renew the proposition heretofore submitted by the Vermont Central Railroad Company to the Rutland and Burlington Railroad Company, to refer the whole matter to disinterested persons, to be agreed upon by the parties, or to enter into any farther negotiation on the subject, so soon as the Directors of the Rutland and Burlington shall have full power to act in the matter.

Very respectfully, your obedient servant,

CHARLES PAINE, *for the Committee.*

[COPY.]

"The Rutland and Burlington Railroad Company, reserving to themselves, at all times, the right of constructing their extension from Burlington, as specified in the Charter of 1850, propose to make an equal division of the joint earnings of the Rutland and Burlington and the Vermont Central, to and from the competing points on both roads, as the same now exist, and also as they may be found to exist after the construction of said extension, should it be made.

"The arrangement for such division to continue from one to fifty years, at the pleasure of the Vermont Central Railroad. Six months' notice to be given by the Vermont Central of their pleasure to discontinue the same.

T. Follett, *President.*

Boston, January 3, 1851."

Mr. Sturgis, in offering this Report, remarked that it was made in this form because the Committee were unable to recommend any action, in the present attitude of the two parties, (the Rutland and the Vermont Central,) that would be of any effect. He felt confident that at no distant day an arrangement would be made between those parties; and he formed his opinion on the fact, obvious to every one, that their own interests demanded it.

On his motion, the Committee was then discharged from any farther consideration of the subject.

Judge Follett referred to the fact that a Report had been made, partially, by this same Committee, upon the division existing between the parties, and that on that day the Rutland road had assented, officially, by direction of the Board of Directors, to the proposition made to them by the Committee. He supposed that the disposition of the Vermont Central Railroad was not known, until to-day, in Committee, as it had been read to the Convention in the documents accompanying the Report. Therefore, he had considered the subject as standing open until to-day. The objections made in the answer of the Vermont Central road, that it might be bound by the arrangement to an indefinite period, while the Rutland road could reject it to-morrow, were obviated by the proposition of the latter road, which also accompanied the Report. The Vermont Central road offered to submit the matter to referees, but he thought there was some ambiguity in the offer; it might be in reference to the rate at which a division should be made. He had asked to-day if the building of the Swanton road was included in the proposition, and Gov. Paine had said that it was. That matter was not and could not be submitted to any reference; the Rutland road must have the sole decision.

He regretted the absence of Gov. Paine, as he wished to say that that gentleman had utterly misunderstood him in supposing him to offer to postpone the building of the Swanton road, much less, postpone it for two years. He never intended to hint at such a thing. The idea of such postponement was not brought into the question, and never was in his mind, whatever might have been Gov. Paine's impression.

Mr. Sturgis said that Judge Follett assumed that the proposition was confined to the recommendation of the Committee. He could not say what was Gov. Paine's intention, but his words were, "he would refer the whole matter." But previously, Judge F. had said that the Directors of the Rutland road had no power over the fate of the Swanton road. So, whatever had been Gov. Paine's intention, his proposition for a reference had been made after and with a knowledge of this fact. Gov. Paine had also said that he did not consider that matter of the Swanton road as of any consequence.

Mr. Rice, of the *Rutland Railroad*, explained his only object in speaking on this question (on the fifth day of meeting) to have been the wish to state, in Judge Follett's absence, what he had heard from him as to the arrangements.

Mr. Howe, of the *Boston and Maine Railroad*, still

hoping for some arrangement between the parties, proposed that the Report should be accepted without farther discussion.

Mr. Linsley, of the ***Rutland Railroad***, made an explanation similar in its tenor to that just made, and substantiating that of Judge Follett.

The Report was then accepted.

Mr. Linsley then called up the second Resolution of the Committee on the subject of raising the rates of fare, &c.

Mr. Higginson moved, and it was voted, to amend the Resolution by adding, between the words "would" and "naturally," the words, "in the ordinary course of trade." (p. 109.)

Mr. Chandler, of the *Northern N. Y. (Ogdensburg) Railroad*, said that this Resolution would not help that road with the New York Legislature. It would not be believed that New England people had expended thirty million dollars in Railroads, without intending or wishing to compete with the internal improvements of New York. No Tariff was ever made up without reference to competition. In making that for the Ogdensburg road, he had had reference to competition, even with the local trade and with the Erie and Welland canals. In respect to the latter, he had even agreed to pay tolls on vessels bringing to his road their freights. He meant, if he could, to enter into competition with the water transportation on the St. Lawrence River, up and down. On the article of Salt, he had entered into competition, and next year meant to take British Salt at $2.00 per ton, and so get return freights for his cars. This Resolution, he thought, struck at the root of all competition, and was therefore unsound. Besides, the plan would prove useless; the roads would not adhere to it, if it were passed.

Mr. Higginson thought that Mr. Chandler mistook the whole purport of the Resolution. The Report admitted, in effect, that competition was inevitable; but many believed that business enough could be obtained without competing with the low rates of freight to New York city. It was difficult to determine what was really a remunerative price. The first Report excepted the great staples of the West, and he was willing now to except these, but not the freight originating on Lake Champlain, because (as had been fully stated) if the rates of freight from Burlington to Boston were put down low enough to meet the water communication with New York, it would operate on all the intermediate roads, lowering all the rates between Burlington and the Merrimack valley. It was not good policy to reduce all the rates of way freight, for the small profit on the through freight. He knew that the gentlemen of the Rutland road would see with regret freight going down to New York without their competition, but he thought they would be better satisfied not to lose the large profits on their other business, in attempting to secure the small profits on this.

Mr. Chandler did not think the upper roads had any right to dictate to the lower ones. They should work together, and only for profit. This discussion, at any rate, would do good. He thought the subject might be referred to a Committee, with power to settle the rates of freight between Boston and Rouse's Point. He wished sincerely for some settlement, for he was asked almost every day what was the cost of freight to Boston, and had been thus far unable to answer. If the gentlemen interested would come to some agreement, and settle on a fair Tariff, he was sure it would benefit both them and the Ogdensburg road.

Mr. CONANT questioned the utility of all this discussion, inasmuch as the freights were not now too low. On the Rutland road, they were as high as on the Western, taking the grades and other things into consideration. The freight on Manganese, which could be procured in Vermont, on the line of the Rutland road, was so high as to be perfectly prohibitory; the freight from the sea coast to Europe was less than that to Boston. The article, consequently, was not mined, and therefore, for all its value, lay useless in the bowels of the earth. He could not agree with the doctrines of the Resolutions, and would take such articles, if only at twenty-five cents a ton profit.

Mr. CHANDLER observed that, in his opinion, sufficient discrimination was not made between large and small quantities of freight. He had rather carry freight in large lots for $3.00, than in small lots at $5.00; there was, generally, a difference in expense and trouble of at least fifty per cent.

Mr. HIGGINSON stated that he had an amendment to offer to the Resolution, and moved to lay it temporarily on the table, which was carried.

Mr. HOWE then moved, and it was voted,

"That Messrs. Thacher, Felton and Higginson be a Committee to consider the subject of printing the proceedings of this Convention.

"And that they be authorized to cause the whole (or such part as they think desirable) to be printed, for the use of the Convention.

"And that they be also authorized to audit the bills for the expenses of the Convention, and assess the proportion of expense upon each road represented in the Convention."

This was agreed to, unanimously.

Mr. Hale, of the *Cheshire Railroad*, then called up the Resolution offered by Judge Gove, in the name of Judge Upham. (p. 114.)

After considerable discussion, and several amendments and reconsiderations, this Resolution was finally amended, by general consent, so as to stand as follows, in which form it was unanimously adopted:—

Resolved, That this Convention recommend that a Committee, consisting of one from each of the following roads, viz.:

The Rutland, Cheshire, Vermont and Massachusetts, and Fitchburg, on the one line; and

The Vermont Central, Concord, Nashua, and Boston and Maine, on the other line,

Be appointed, to agree on and recommend rates of freight between Boston and Burlington, whether Western or local freight, and to confer with a Committee for the Ogdensburg road, as to the rate of freight between Ogdensburg and Boston."

On motion of Mr. Higginson, the vote fixing the day of meeting of the Central Board was reconsidered, and it was

Voted, That the first meeting of the Central Board be held on the Wednesday next preceding the last

Wednesday in February next, at the Superintendent's Room, No. 11½ Tremont Row, Boston.

On motion of Mr. HALE, of the *Cheshire Railroad*, it was

Voted, That the Secretary be directed to send a copy of the Resolution for a Committee to fix the rates of freight to the roads interested.

Voted, That the time of meeting of this Committee be fixed at 10, A. M., on the last Wednesday of January, at the Superintendent's Room, No. 11½ Tremont Row, Boston.

A motion was then made, but withdrawn, that when the Convention adjourn, it adjourn until to-morrow morning.

Judge FOLLETT asked for some information as to the powers and duties of the Central Board.

Mr. HIGGINSON replied by reading from the minutes of the Convention and the Report of the Committee.

Mr. DERBY thought that the powers granted to the Committee were too great.

Judge FOLLETT agreed with this, and thought the roads would object to sending delegates, on these terms.

Mr. LINSLEY moved, and it was voted, to strike out the clause in the Report intrusting powers to delegates; but, after some conversation respecting the propriety of altering the records of the Secretary, this vote was *reconsidered*.

Mr. HIGGINSON moved the following: —

Voted, That, with a view to prevent misunderstanding, the authority of the delegates to the Central Board, as provided by the vote of December 13, shall be such only as may be given by special vote of the Directors sending such delegates.

Judge Follett thought that some Boards would hesitate to send delegates, even should this vote be passed.

The motion was then agreed to.

Some conversation then took place between Messrs. Higginson, Derby and Follett as to the calling of future Conventions. Judge Follett thought they were beneficial, and hoped they would be frequent. Mr. Higginson said that he supposed a part of the duty of the Central Board would be to call Conventions, when expedient.

Mr. Linsley moved, and it was voted, that when the Convention adjourn, it adjourn *sine die.*

On motion of Mr. Higginson, it was

Voted, That the Committee on publishing the records of this Convention be authorized, if necessary, to substitute Mr. Tilton in place of Mr. Felton, on their Committee.

On motion of Mr. Linsley, it was

Resolved, That the thanks of this Convention be presented to Hon. Erastus Fairbanks for the able and impartial manner in which he has presided over its deliberations.

The President made an appropriate reply.

On motion of Dr. Walker, it was

Resolved, That the thanks of this Convention be tendered to the Secretary and Reporter for their close and careful attention to their duties.

On motion of Mr. Linsley, the Convention then adjourned, *sine die.*

Delegates to the Convention.

FITCHBURG RAILROAD.

Jacob Forster,
Israel Longley,
Alvah Crocker,
E. H. Derby,
Dr. H. Adams,
S. M. Felton, *Sup't.*

VERMONT AND MASSACHUSETTS.

Thomas Whittemore,
J. J. Swift,
James Ellison,
Daniel Butterfield, Jr.,
Henry Chapman,
Columbus Tyler,
D. S. Jones, *Sup't.*

CHESHIRE.

Thomas Thacher,
Hiram Hosman,
Salma Hale,
B. F. Adams,
E. Murdock, Jr.,
George Huntington,
T. M. Edwards,
L. Tilton, *Sup't.*

CONCORD AND CLAREMONT.

Joseph Low,
A. Colby,
N. A. Davis.

CONTOOCOOK VALLEY.

James Boyd, J. A. Potter.

NASHUA AND LOWELL.

Daniel Abbott,
Jesse Bowers,
Thomas B. Wales,
Henry Timmins,
William Boardman,
Charles F. Gove, *Sup't.*

BOSTON AND MAINE.

John Howe,
Southworth Shaw,
Samuel Bachelder,
Thomas S. Williams, *Sup't.*

BOSTON AND LOWELL.

William Sturgis,
Joseph Tilden,
Waldo Higginson, *Agent.*

RUTLAND AND BURLINGTON.

Timothy Follett,
George T. Hodges,
Nathan Rice,
Charles Linsley,
John A. Conant,
J. Warner,
C. Granger,
John Bradley,
L. Bigelow, *Sup't.*

CONCORD.

Isaac Spaulding,
Uriel Crocker,
Emmons Raymond,
Josiah Stickney,
N. G. Upham, *Sup't.*

SULLIVAN.

Charles Thompson, J. B. Upham,
George Denny, Aurelius Dickinson,
Jones Livingston, Henry Hubbard, Jr.,
D. A. Gage, *Sup't.*

CONNECTICUT AND PASSUMPSIC.

Erastus Fairbanks, Asa Low,
Addison Gilmore, Oliver Dean,
William Thomas, Arthur Latham,
B. B. Mussey, J. Sawyer,
William F. Weld, Elijah Cleveland,
Fitzhenry Homer, L. H. Deland,
E. Raymond, J. C. Lee,
Robert Hale, *Sup't.*

VERMONT CENTRAL.

Charles Paine, John P. Putnam,
James R. Langdon, James C. Dunn,
Charles O. Whitmore, E. P. Walton,
John Smith, James Moore, *Sup't.*

NORTHERN, N. H.

Josiah B. French, John R. Brown,
Joseph B. Walker, Timothy Kenrick,
George A. Kettell, William J. Walker,
Onslow Stearns, *Sup't.*

NORTHERN, N. Y.—(OGDENSBURG.)

T. P. Chandler, James H. Titus, of N. Y.

MANCHESTER AND LAWRENCE.

Theodore Atkinson, *Sup't.*

WHITE MOUNTAINS—(Not yet in operation.)

Ira Goodall.

VERMONT AND CANADA.

John H. Peck, John Smith, *President*,*
H. R. Campbell, *Engineer*, Charles Paine.*

CHAMPLAIN AND ST. LAWRENCE.

A. H. Brainerd, *Sup't.*

BOSTON AND WORCESTER.

Thomas Hopkinson, Genery Twichell, *Sup't.*

BOSTON AND PROVIDENCE.

Charles H. Warren, W. Raymond Lee, *Sup't.*

* Both these gentlemen are Directors of, and represent also, the Vermont Central Railroad.

www.ingramcontent.com/pod-product-compliance
Lightning Source LLC
LaVergne TN
LVHW021420110826
845150LV00007B/2002

* 9 7 8 1 4 2 5 5 0 9 3 2 3 *